D0115862

NO MORE WORK

JAMES LIVINGSTON

No More
WORK

WHY FULL EMPLOYMENT
IS A BAD IDEA

The University of North Carolina Press
Chapel Hill

This book was published with the assistance of the Anniversary Fund of the University of North Carolina Press.

Designed and set by Jamison Cockerham
Set in Scala, designed by Martin Majoor

Jacket illustration: *Horizontal Breaking Paperclip Chain on Yellow,* © Vince Clements/Shutterstock.com.

Manufactured in the United States of America

The University of North Carolina Press has been a member of the Green Press Initiative since 2003.

LIBRARY OF CONGRESS CATALOGING-IN-PUBLICATION DATA
Names: Livingston, James, 1949–
Title: No more work : why full employment
    is a bad idea / James Livingston.
Description: Chapel Hill: The University of North Carolina
    Press, [2016] | "This book was published with the assistance
    of the Anniversary Fund of the University of North
    Carolina Press." | Includes bibliographical references.
Identifiers: LCCN 2016018226 | ISBN 9781469630656
    (cloth : alk. paper) | ISBN 9781469630663 (ebook)
Subjects: LCSH: Work—Social aspects—United States.
    | Employees—United States—Attitudes.
Classification: LCC HD8045 .L58 2016 | DDC 331.12/0424—dc23
    LC record available at https://lccn.loc.gov/2016018226

This book is for Laura, just her

CONTENTS

PREFACE

I

I've been working my whole life. That's probably why I wrote this book—I'm sick of it. Don't get me wrong, I have two more books in progress, and I like to teach. Besides, my 401k needs replenishing after the Great Recession and my ex-wife's raids on it. Still, I wish I didn't have to work. Or want to.

This book is a kind of sequel to my last one, *Against Thrift*, which readers treated—perhaps correctly—as a schizophrenic mix of economic history and moral philosophy. (It's free as an e-book, so go ahead and download it.) From the Left, I got approval for the history because it demonstrated the economic decrepitude and ethical imbecility of contemporary capitalism. From the same quarter, though, I got disapproval for the philosophy because it suggested that consumer culture is a moral universe superior to the one grounded in the production of goods—the one located on the scene of work. From the Right, well, I got disapproval all around, on the grounds that capitalism is good and consumer culture is bad, as if these phenomena aren't connected.[1]

In this book, I assume the validity of the economic argument I made in *Against Thrift*, and broaden my indictment of the moral universe where we must earn our keep if we're to be true to ourselves — where "meaningful work" and the production of goods is somehow better for us than indolent leisure and the consumption of goods.

The refrain to which this book returns again and again is brutally simple: Fuck Work. That was the original title. This isn't just a cute slogan. It's an orientation toward the future that we must adopt in the name of mere sanity. Our productivity is killing us. It's time we said "No more work — enough."

But in using the f-word, am I belittling what most of us know as the place where our individual character has been built and where our future significance, for better or worse, will be inscribed? Look at all the hard work that needs to be done, all the teaching of children and the rebuilding of rotted infrastructure. Fuck that? Look at what we *learn by doing*, by making things, by producing the world we inhabit rather than passively consuming goods made by others. Fuck that, too?

No, to all of the above. There's plenty of socially beneficial work to do, but it's no longer socially necessary, which means it doesn't pay. The labor market is broken, and it can't be fixed. Or it's been *perfected* at this outer edge of very late capitalism, where the "elasticity of substitution" between capital and labor — between machines and real, live human beings — approaches equivalence. Translation: we lost our race with the machine, but in doing so we won our freedom from the iron grip of economic necessity.

Ask yourself, why is information free? Music? Movies? My answer in this book is that socially necessary labor time has become or is becoming worthless, at least insofar as the price system can signify its value. One way or the other—the labor market is either broken or perfected—work can't serve as the disciplinary groundwork of your character or the legitimate source of your income or the proper register of your life's worth. So, let's be realistic: Fuck it.

II

Once upon a time, the Protestant work ethic was a leveling, democratizing attitude and social force. It served as a critique of aristocratic exemption from necessary labor because it insisted that everybody had to justify their consumption of goods by their prior production of value—everybody. But from the beginning, with Luther's insistence on a "calling," it was a kind of "slave morality," as Hegel, Marx, Nietzsche, and Freud agreed, each in his own way. It justified renunciation and abstention from the present in the name of the future: "saving for a rainy day," in the vernacular, storing up those sacrificed possibilities in the hope that redemption—sacred or secular, entering heaven or cashing out—would follow.

So, when I say Fuck Work, I mean that it no longer functions as either a moral calendar or an economic calculator. You will learn nothing about character by going to work at the minimum wage because the gangsters or the morons at corporate headquarters control your opportunities; you will learn nothing about the rationality of the market because the same people determine your income.

I also mean that the slave morality of renunciation and abstention has outlived its usefulness. It's obsolete for the obvious reason that if we keep working as hard as we can, producing as much as do, we'll incinerate the planet. Beyond that—is there such a thing?—the deferment of gratification that we call work has by now become more repression than sublimation. It doesn't merely delay and redirect our desires into socially useful channels; it mutilates them. Once upon a time, going or getting to work was a way of discovering and developing your capacities. By now it's become a way to avoid yourself.

By saying Fuck Work, I mean—finally—to say that since the correlation of income and work is already incomprehensible and unjustifiable, we need to decouple them, in accordance with what transfer payments, "entitlements," Wall Street bonuses, and real-life experiments with a guaranteed income have taught us—*that, for better or worse, getting something for nothing has no measurable effect on the character of the recipients.*

That empirical fact propels us into a moral universe where work can't serve as a reliable index of anything about you. Except that, like me, you have to.

In this book, I won't detain you with the economic history that freighted the last one. But I do think the rudiments are worth reviewing. So, here are the Cliff/Spark Notes on the economics of my argument. It won't take you long, I promise.

Once upon a time, in the nineteenth century, economic growth was driven by net additions to the capital stock and to the labor force. In other words, growth was built on more machines — "physical plant and equipment," they call it — and more workers operating those machines. In the parlance of economists, net private investment rose, capital stock per worker increased, and both employment and labor force participation rates did, too. Much of that investment took the material form of labor-saving machinery — plant and equipment that displaced workers — but *somebody had to build the machinery*, so overall demand for labor kept rising.

Since 1919, growth has worked differently. Thereafter, net private investment declined, and employment in goods production did, too, but growth didn't stop, not even in the 1930s. These trends have persisted for almost a hundred years. What follows?

If growth no longer requires new additions to the capital stock, or net private investment — which simply means using profits to purchase new plant and equipment, also to pay the labor force to operate it — corporate profits become pointless, superfluous, even dangerous, because they can't be reinvested in productive ways. They're surplus capital, nothing more, nothing less. Consequently, speculative bubbles and financial crises become the normal, predictable pattern of economic development, not surprising deviations from market equilibrium.

If growth no longer requires net additions to the labor force, work itself can't be justified by the invocation of economic necessity, and income must be decoupled from work—full employment becomes a fool's errand.

And if growth requires neither more capital nor more labor, less work and more leisure become the key not just to the good life, as John Maynard Keynes insisted, but to life as such.

So if we want to save the planet, and with it, ourselves, we need to work less, not more. That's what I mean when I say Fuck Work!

NO MORE WORK

Introduction

I

Work means everything to us. For centuries—since, say, 1650—we've believed that it builds character (punctuality, initiative, honesty, self-discipline, and so forth). We've also believed that the market in labor, where we go to find work, has been relatively efficient in allocating opportunities and incomes. And we've believed that even if it sucks, the job gives meaning, purpose, and structure to our everyday lives—at any rate we're pretty sure that it gets us out of bed, pays the bills, makes us feel responsible, and keeps us away from daytime TV.

These beliefs are no longer plausible. In fact, they've become ridiculous, because there's not enough work to go around, and what there is of it won't pay the bills—unless, of course, you've landed a job as a drug dealer or a Wall Street banker, becoming a gangster either way.

These days everybody from Left to Right—from Dean Baker

to Arthur C. Brooks—addresses this breakdown of the labor market by advocating full employment, as if having a job is self-evidently a good thing, no matter how dangerous, demanding, or demeaning it is. But "full employment" is not the way to restore our faith in hard work, or playing by the rules, or whatever (note that the official unemployment rate is already below 6 percent, which is pretty close to what economists used to call full employment). Shitty jobs for everyone won't solve any social problem we now face.

Don't take my word for it, look at the numbers. Already a fourth of the adults *actually employed* in the United States are paid wages lower than would lift them above the official poverty line—and so a fourth of American children live in poverty. Almost half of *employed* adults in this country are eligible for food stamps (most of those who are eligible don't apply). The market in labor has broken down along with most others.

Those jobs that disappeared in the Great Recession just aren't coming back, regardless of what the unemployment rate tells you—the net gain in jobs since 2000 still stands at zero—and if they do return from the dead they'll be zombies, those contingent, part-time, or minimum-wage jobs where the bosses shuffle your shift from week to week: welcome to Walmart, where food stamps are a benefit.

And don't tell me that raising the minimum wage to $15 an hour solves the problem. No one can doubt the moral significance of the movement. But at this rate of pay, even at forty hours a week—an unlikely amount in fast-food franchises—you're still at that official poverty line. What, exactly, is the point of a earning a paycheck that isn't a living wage, except to prove that you have a work ethic?

But isn't our present dilemma just a passing phase of the business cycle? What about the job market of the future? Haven't the doomsayers, those damn Malthusians, always been proved wrong by rising productivity, new fields of enterprise, new economic opportunities? Well, yeah—until now, these times. The measurable trends of the past half century, and the plausible projections for the next half century, are just too empirically grounded to dismiss as dismal science or ideological hokum. They look like the data on climate change—you can deny them if you like, but you'll sound like a moron when you do.

Oxford economists who study employment trends tell us that fully two-thirds of existing jobs, including those involving "non-routine cognitive tasks"—you know, like *thinking*—are at risk of death by computerization within twenty years. They're elaborating on conclusions reached by two MIT economists in a book from 2012 called *Race against the Machine*. Meanwhile, the Silicon Valley types who give TED talks have started speaking of "surplus humans" as a result of the same process—cybernated production. *Rise of the Robots*, the title of a new book that cites these very sources, is social science, not science fiction.[1]

So this Great Recession of ours is a moral crisis as well as an economic catastrophe. You might even say it's a spiritual impasse, because it makes us ask what social scaffolding other than work will permit the construction of character—or whether character itself is something we must aspire to. But that is why it's also an intellectual opportunity: it forces us to imagine a world in which the job no longer builds our character, determines our incomes, or dominates our daily lives.

In short, it lets us say, "Enough already; fuck work."

II

Certainly this crisis makes us ask what comes *after* work? What would you do without your job as the external discipline that organizes your waking life—as the social imperative that gets you up and on your way to the factory, the office, the store, the warehouse, the restaurant, wherever you work, and, no matter how much you hate it, keeps you coming back? What would you do if you didn't have to work to receive an income?

And what would society and civilization be like if we didn't have to *earn* a living—if leisure was not our choice but our lot? Would we hang out at the local Starbucks, laptops open? Or volunteer to teach children in less-developed countries, like Mississippi? Or smoke weed and watch reality TV all day?

I'm not proposing a fancy thought experiment here. By now these are *practical* questions because there aren't enough jobs. So it's time we asked even more practical questions. How do you make a living *without a job*—can you receive income without working for it? Is it possible, to begin with, and then the hard part: Is it ethical? If you were raised to believe that work is the index of your value to society—most of us were—would it feel like cheating to get something for nothing?

We already have some provisional answers because we're all on the dole, more or less. The fastest-growing component of household income since 1959 has been "transfer payments" from government. By the turn of the twenty-first century, 20 percent of *all* household income came from this source—from what is otherwise known as welfare or "entitlements." Without this income supplement, *half* of the adults with full-time jobs would live below the poverty line, and *most* working Americans would be eligible for food stamps.

But are these transfer payments and entitlements affordable, in either economic or moral terms? By continuing and enlarging them, do we subsidize sloth, or do we enrich a debate on the rudiments of the good life?

Transfer payments or "entitlements," not to mention Wall Street bonuses—talk about getting something for nothing—have taught us how to detach the receipt of income from the production of goods, but now, in plain view of the end of work, the lesson needs rethinking. No matter how you calculate the federal budget, we can afford to be our brother's keeper. The real question is not whether but how we choose to be.

III

I know what you're thinking—we can't afford this! But, yeah, we can, very easily. We raise the arbitrary lid on the Social Security contribution, which now stands at $113,700, and we raise taxes on corporate income, reversing the Reagan

Revolution. These two steps solve a fake fiscal problem and create an economic surplus where we now can measure a moral deficit.

Of course you will say, along with every economist from Dean Baker to Greg Mankiw, Left to Right, that raising taxes on corporate income is a disincentive to investment and thus job creation. Or that it will drive corporations overseas, where taxes are lower.

But in fact raising taxes on corporate income *can't* have these effects.

Let's work backward. Corporations have been multinational for quite some time. In the 1970s and 1980s, before Reagan's signature tax cuts took effect, approximately 60 percent of manufactured imported goods were produced offshore, overseas, *by U.S. companies.* That percentage has risen since then, but not by much.

Chinese workers aren't the problem—the homeless, aimless idiocy of corporate accounting is. That is why the *Citizens United* decision of 2010 is hilarious. Money isn't speech, not any more than noise is. The Supreme Court has conjured a living being, a new person, from the remains of the common law, creating a real world more frightening than its cinematic equivalent, say, *Frankenstein, Blade Runner,* or, more recently, *Transformers.*

But the bottom line is this: *most jobs aren't created by private, corporate investment, so raising taxes on corporate income won't affect employment.* You heard me right. Since the 1920s, economic growth has happened even though net private investment has atrophied. What does that mean? It means that profits are pointless except as a way of announcing to your stockholders (and hostile takeover specialists) that your company is a going concern, a thriving business. You don't need profits to reinvest, to finance the expansion of your company's workforce or output, as the recent history of Apple and most other corporations has amply demonstrated.

So investment decisions by CEOs have only a marginal effect on employment. Taxing the profits of corporations to finance a welfare state that permits us to love our neighbors and to be our brother's keeper is not an economic problem. It's something else—it's an intellectual issue, a moral conundrum.

IV

When we place our faith in hard work, we're wishing for the creation of character; but we're also hoping, or expecting, that the labor market will allocate *incomes* fairly and rationally. And there's the rub: they do go together. Character can be created on the job only when we can see that there's an intelligible, justifiable relation between past effort, learned skills, and present reward. When I see that your income is completely out of proportion to your production of real value, of durable goods the rest of us can use and appreciate (and by "durable" I don't mean just material things), I begin to doubt that character is a consequence of hard work.

When I see, for example, that you're making millions by

laundering drug cartel money (HSBC), or pushing bad paper on mutual fund managers (AIG, Bear Stearns, Morgan Stanley, Citibank), or preying on low-income borrowers (Bank of America), or buying votes in Congress (all of the above)—just business as usual on Wall Street—while I'm barely making ends meet from the earnings of my full-time job, I realize that my participation in the labor market is irrational. I know that building my character through work is stupid because crime pays. I might as well become a gangster like you.

That's why an economic crisis like the Great Recession is also a moral problem, a spiritual impasse—and an intellectual opportunity. We've placed so many bets on the social, cultural, and ethical import of work that when the labor market fails, as it so spectacularly has, we're at a loss to explain what happened, or to orient ourselves to a different set of meanings for work and for markets.

And by "we" I mean pretty much all of us, Left to Right, because everybody wants to put Americans back to work, one way or another—full employment is the goal of right-wing politicians no less than left-wing economists. The differences between them are over means, not ends, and those ends include intangibles like the acquisition of character.

Which is to say that everybody has doubled down on the benefits of work just as it reaches a vanishing point. "Full employment" has become a bipartisan goal at the very moment it has become both impossible and unnecessary.

V

Why?

Because work means everything to us—regardless of whether it still produces solid character and allocates incomes rationally, and quite apart from the need to make a living. It's been the medium of most of our thinking about the good life since Plato correlated craftsmanship and the possibility of ideas as such. It's been our way of defying death, by making and repairing the durable things, the significant things we know will last beyond our allotted time on earth because they teach us, as we make or repair them, that the world beyond us—the world before and after us—has its own reality principles.

Think about the scope of this idea. Work has been our way of demonstrating differences between males and females, for example, by merging the meanings of fatherhood and "breadwinner," and then, more recently, prying them apart. Since the seventeenth century, masculinity and femininity have been defined—not necessarily achieved—by their places in a moral economy, as working men were paid wages for their production of value on the job, or as working women were paid nothing for their production and maintenance of families. Of course these definitions are now changing, as the meaning of "family" does, along with profound and parallel changes in the labor market—the entry of women marks just one of those—and in attitudes toward sexuality.

When work disappears, the genders produced by the labor market are blurred. When socially necessary labor declines, what we once called *women's work*—education, health care, service—becomes our basic industry, not a tertiary dimension of the measurable economy. The labor of love, caring for one another and learning how to be our brother's keeper—socially beneficial labor—becomes not merely possible but eminently necessary, and not just within families, where affection is routinely available. No, I mean out there in the wide, wide world.

Work has also been the American way of producing "racial capitalism," as historians now call it, by means of slave labor, convict labor, sharecropping, then segregated labor markets—in other words, a free enterprise system built on the ruins of black bodies, an economic edifice animated, saturated, and determined by racism. *There never was a free market in labor in these United States.* Like every other market, it was always hedged by lawful, systematic discrimination against black folk. You might even say that this hedged market *produced* the still deployed stereotypes of African American laziness by excluding black workers from remunerative employment, confining them to the ghettos of the eight-hour day.

And yet, and yet. Though work has often entailed subjugation, obedience, and hierarchy (see above), it's also where we have consistently expressed our deepest human desire, to be free of externally imposed authority or obligation, to be self-sufficient. We have defined ourselves for centuries by what we do, by what we *produce*.

But by now we must know that this definition of ourselves entails the principle of productivity—from each according to his abilities, to each according to his creation of real value through work—and commits us to the inane idea that we're worth only as much as the market can register. By now we must also know that this principle plots a certain course to endless growth and its faithful attendant, environmental degradation.

Until now, the principle of productivity has functioned as the reality principle that made the American Dream seem plausible. "Work hard, play by the rules, get ahead"; or, "You get what you pay for, you make your own way, you rightly receive what you've honestly earned"—such homilies and exhortations used to make sense of the world. At any rate they didn't sound delusional. By now they do.

Adherence to the principle of productivity therefore threatens public health as well as the planet—by committing us to what is impossible, it makes for madness. A Nobel Prize–winning economist said something like this when he explained anomalous mortality rates among white people in the Bible Belt by claiming they've "lost the narrative of their lives," suggesting they've lost faith in the American Dream. For them, the work ethic is a death sentence because they can't live by it.[2]

So the impending end of work raises the most fundamental questions about what it means to be human. To begin with, what purposes could we choose if the job—economic necessity—didn't consume most of our waking hours and creative energies? What evident yet unknown possibilities would then appear? How would human nature itself change if the ancient, aristocratic privilege of leisure becomes the birthright of human beings as such?

Sigmund Freud insisted that love and work were the

essential ingredients of healthy human being. Of course he was right. But can love survive the end of work as the willing partner of the good life? Can we let people get something for nothing and still treat them as our brothers and sisters—as members of a beloved community? Can you imagine the moment when you've just met an attractive stranger at a party, or you're online looking for someone, anyone, but you don't ask, "So, what do you do?"

We won't have any answers until we acknowledge that work now means everything to us—and that hereafter it can't.

ONE

The Family Assistance Plan and the End of Work

I

On April 17, 1970, the House of Representatives voted 243 to 155 for legislation that would install a guaranteed annual income for all American citizens in need. In so many words, a substantial majority of Congress said, "Fuck work!" Well, almost.

These congressmen weren't utopians fresh from the commune or the campus, nor bumpkins just off the turnip truck. They were serious citizens with good reasons for their votes. They could read the recommendations of three weighty presidential commissions on dealing with the question of unemployment. And they had empirical grounds for supporting Richard Nixon's agenda for welfare reform, what he called his Family Assistance Program (FAP).

Most important, they could rely on the report of an ongoing income-maintenance study supervised by the Office of Economic Opportunity—where Nixon's young guns, Donald Rumsfeld and Dick Cheney, presided.

The archconservatives of our time, Rumsfeld and Cheney, spearheaded the effort to install a guaranteed annual income. What novelist could make this up?

In fact, this was the logical endpoint of a long and tortured debate. From 1910, when William James published "The Moral Equivalent of War," until the 1990s, American writers, artists, and intellectuals studied, celebrated, and worried over the impending end of work; meanwhile politicians wondered what to do about it. The lyrical Left and the political mainstream pondered the same problem, or promise: what happens when the work runs out?

Today the Left, broadly construed to include socialists, liberals, and all manner of intermediate positions, has just one answer: full employment. So does the Right, broadly construed to include libertarians, conservatives, evangelicals, and the ample bandwidth in between. All parties want, above all, to create more jobs.

But forty-five years ago, the Left and the Right agreed on the *other* answer. To repeat, on April 17, 1970, the House of Representatives voted decisively for legislation that would install a guaranteed annual income for all American citizens in need. Those members of Congress were finally persuaded by a report from the Office of Economic Opportunity (OEO), where Donald Rumsfeld and Dick Cheney presided.

The OEO study was the brainchild of Heather Ross, a Ph.D. candidate in economics at MIT. It was an academic's dream: a dissertation proposal turned into federal policy. Ross wanted to conduct a real-life social experiment that could answer the most basic questions raised by transfer payments (what we now call "entitlements"). Would people continue to work if the government guaranteed them enough income to stay above the poverty line? Or would they become laggards and layabouts perfectly happy with their dependence on the dole?

Ross's colleagues at the Brookings Institution, where she was a fellow in 1967, forwarded the proposal to their acquaintances at OEO, which then offered to fund the experiment and hired the Institute for Research on Poverty at the University of Wisconsin to staff it. Ross participated in the study as a consultant to Mathematica Policy Research, a Princeton think tank already under contract to the Institute at Wisconsin. But she ultimately reported to her boss, James O. Wilson, the research director at OEO, and to his bosses there — Rumsfeld and Cheney, who would shape the study to vouch for Nixon's FAP.

The dissertation Ross had devised was eventually called the "New Jersey Graduated Work Incentive Experiment." Note that title: a guaranteed income poses as a work incentive: the doublespeak permitted a political latitude that went missing in the 1980s. This study became the template for four other social experiments, each of them designed and executed on a grander scale. Three were conducted in the United States — in Gary,

Seattle, Denver, and low-income rural counties in Iowa and North Carolina, between 1969 and 1982. The fourth and most ambitious was conducted in Manitoba, Canada, in the little town of Dauphin, from 1974 to 1979, about which more later.

The so-called New Jersey Experiment studied low-income families in "declining urban areas": 1,357 male-headed households in all, from Trenton, Passaic, Paterson, Jersey City, and, mysteriously, Scranton, Pennsylvania—had New Jersey annexed the anthracite districts?—over a three-year period beginning in 1968. The typical income supplement for this experimental group, which was evenly balanced by race, was $1,100, raising its average family income to $5,348 (in 2014 dollars, roughly $32,000). The control group lived on that much less, right around the official poverty line of $4,000.[1]

Would the subsidized men and women work less? Would getting something for nothing change their attitude, their character, their work ethic?

The interim report detailing this inaugural study was issued by Rumsfeld's OEO in 1970. It contained what now seem startling results, which would nevertheless be *ratified by every study that followed*, including the largest and the longest of the five, the Seattle-Denver survey of 1971–1982, which covered 4,800 families.[2]

The most important of those results was that "work effort" in the experimental group—*the one getting something for nothing* —barely changed: "There is no evidence that work effort declined among those receiving income support payments. On the contrary [!], there is an indication that the work effort of

The Family Assistance Plan and the End of Work

participants receiving payments increased relative to the work effort of those not receiving payments."

In the New Jersey Experiment, for example, the husbands cut their work week by slightly less than an hour (and the proportional reductions were the same for Gary, Seattle, and Denver). The wives cut five hours off their work week, but they spent that "free" time with their many children—the average family size in the New Jersey study was 5.8—particularly, it seems, to help them with homework after school.

The women *reduced* their labor force participation rates as nominal family income rose, in other words, choosing more time over more income, in an exact inversion of what has happened in the workplace since the 1980s. When given a choice, the working mothers leaned in to spend time with their children, probably because their husbands weren't going to pitch in with household chores anyway.

All the while, at the OEO, Rumsfeld and Cheney were running interference for Nixon's Family Assistance Program, which included substantial provisions for subsidized day care and job training, *as well as* income-support payments for low-income households. So the report of 1970, *Preliminary Results of the New Jersey Graduated Work Incentive Experiment*, emphasized that its findings made the administration's FAP eminently practical, not utopian or radical: "We believe that these preliminary data suggest that fears that a Family Assistance Plan could result in extreme, unusual, or unanticipated responses are unfounded."

What's more, it would be cheaper than welfare: "The Family Assistance Program, excluding the Day Care Program and

Work Training Provisions, can be administered at an annual cost per family of $72 to $96. Similar costs for the current welfare system run between $200 and $300 annually per family."[3]

According to Fred Cook, who summarized this preliminary report in a long piece for the *New York Times Magazine* which bordered on disbelief—they did what in New Jersey?!—it "profoundly influenced" the vote in the House on April 17.[4]

III

You have to sympathize with Cook's incredulity. What were these people thinking?

These were the men who would soon become the archetypes of neoconservatism—or neoliberalism. Out of office, they would design what they called the Project for a New American Century. Back in power under George W. Bush, they would destroy every valuable remnant of that century by acting as if military power is the only measurable kind. What made their radical experiments and remarkable legislation seem justifiable in 1970?

It's not as weird as it looks in retrospect. And it's not to be explained by the triumph of free market ideology. The liberals bailed first on Nixon's project, in 1970, and they did so in the name of family values, long before the conservatives seized on that issue. Daniel Patrick Moynihan didn't exactly lead the way when he decided that a guaranteed annual income was no better than existing welfare programs because it, too, promoted the dissolution of families, and, as a result, reproduced a "culture of poverty." But his doubts fed into the eventual stall of the FAP in the Senate.

Notice three salient features of the experiments and the legislation. First, they were designed to *replace* welfare and to preserve the integrity of the *family*, which in the minds of most legislators, Democrats or Republicans, were the same thing. The big idea here was to abolish the perceived disincentives to marriage in the Aid to Families with Dependent Children program by making it easier for households and harder for single parents to acquire an adequate income.

Second, the experiments and the legislation provided income *supplements* to the working poor, rather than grants or a baseline sum to everyone, or to people without jobs. The point—the result—of the experiments was to show that time on the job didn't decline as income without work increased, *not* to discourage job-seeking or steady employment; the legislation of 1970 that called for income supplements, Nixon's Family Assistance Program, took these findings for granted.

Even George McGovern's counterproposal, the famous manifesto of May 4, 1972 (published in the *New York Review of Books*), which would have given all Americans a minimum income grant, made the "loss of grant benefits [as family income rose] sufficiently gradual as not to discourage those on welfare from seeking a job." *So the full-employment agenda was already the default setting of the Democratic Party* and the larger Left produced by the New Deal coalition. When he proposed an increase in the corporate income tax rate, for example,

McGovern emphasized that his program also included a $10 billion fiscal stimulus that would enhance consumer spending *and* corporate profits: "Nothing spurs profits like a strong full employment economy, which has the highest priority in my economic program."[5]

Third, and this is most important for my purposes, everyone assumed that wages for work would soon be insufficient to sustain family life. Manufacturing jobs were already disappearing as North America underwent the late stages of "automation" —what we now call the early stages of "computerization." The end of work was visible, indeed measurable, back in the 1960s, and the people who acted on this knowledge, among them Heather Ross and her bosses at the Office of Economic Opportunity, wanted to know what would happen to the moral fabric woven into the American Dream when a man's job wasn't the principal source of his family's income.

But they didn't just speculate and pontificate about it. They converted it into a social question to be answered with empirical detail. *They wanted to know whether family and character were attainable when work was not.*

In this sense, the social experiments pioneered by Heather Ross, sponsored by Donald Rumsfeld and Dick Cheney at the OEO, then approved by a majority of the House of Representatives, were answers to questions that journalists and intellectuals had been asking since the 1920s, when we all fell behind in that race with the machine.

Would the work ethic disappear along with work itself? How would you claim your fair share of goods available in the market if your job didn't afford you reasonable compensation—or if you didn't even have a job, through no fault of your own? Is moral discipline a result of economic necessity, the kind we call "work"?

In the 1930s, of course, these questions acquired a practical, unbearable urgency. But *before and after* the Great Depression, they were the stock-in-trade of journalists, academics, and intellectuals, because just about everybody had the end of work already in their sights. In the 1920s, the net loss of jobs in manufacturing amounted to 2 million—and neither Chinese nor Mexican factories were to blame.

I've written elsewhere about this process. But maybe it's worth rehearsing here, as preparation for the startling revelations to follow. Non-farm labor productivity and output increased 40 and 60 percent, respectively, in the 1920s, but non-farm employment in goods production declined. Why? Because socially necessary labor time was also declining—because for the first time in history, less so-called past labor, capital goods congealed in the material form of plant and equipment, was required to produce more at lower cost. How? Because technological innovation, "the machine," was already extricating "living labor," workers themselves, from goods production.

The people who designed and conducted and summarized the great social experiments of the late 1960s and 1970s understood this process, this predicament—these people, among them Rumsfeld and Cheney, knew that unemployment was a long-term, structural problem that went back to the 1920s, when economists first noticed that gains in labor productivity would no longer increase demand for labor, and that full employment had become a function of public spending, mostly on war.

So they asked how to redistribute income, and how to promote consumer spending and economic growth, maybe marriage and family too, *by reducing work hours and subsidizing incomes.* Beyond that, they asked what the effect of less work and more income would be on the character of those who got something for nothing.

IV

In doing so, these people weren't ahead of their time — though they're certainly ahead of ours. They were reading (or listening to, or consulting with) the journalists, academics, and intellectuals of their moment. Many were measuring what they called a postindustrial civilization, a consumer culture, an economy of abundance, or an affluent society — almost interchangeable designations by the 1960s — and meanwhile warning that, in this new phase of human development, work was already a waning dimension of everyday life.

These were the leading lights in their respective fields, and their political affiliations were various, to say the least. Among them were the economists Milton Friedman, George Stigler, Wassily Leontief, John Kenneth Galbraith, Eli Ginzberg, Harold Vatter, and Lawrence R. Klein (four Nobel Prize winners among them); the sociologists Daniel Bell, C. Wright Mills, and

Michael Harrington; the historians Richard Hofstadter, David Potter, and William Appleman Williams; the philosophers Herbert Marcuse, Norman O. Brown, and Hannah Arendt.

In 1956, for example, Daniel Bell, the man responsible for the concept of postindustrial society, declared that "not only the worker but *work itself* is being displaced by the machine," and worried about the social and moral consequences. This was when jobs in manufacturing—autos and steel, for example —remained plentiful yet constituted a small and shrinking proportion of jobs as such. "Tertiary" employment (trade, finance/insurance, services, government) already represented 60 percent of all jobs, roughly three times the proportion of those in goods production. Then, over the next eight years, manufacturing output doubled, while the number of jobs in goods production (aka blue-collar workers) declined. Automation was particularly effective in autos and steel: Detroit and Pittsburgh would soon be ghost towns.[6]

By 1964, the displacement of labor by automation and cybernated technologies (computerization) had become a public issue worthy of both a presidential commission and a manifesto from Students for a Democratic Society (the latter was called "America and the New World")—in fact, the two overlapped because the origin of the commission was an open letter to the president from the "Ad Hoc Committee on the Triple Revolution [Cybernetics, Weaponry, Human Rights]" dated March 22, 1964, which was signed by, among other dignitaries, Todd Gitlin, Tom Hayden, and Michael Harrington.

The key passages from the open letter are these: "The

fundamental problem posed by the cybernation revolution in the US is that it invalidates the general mechanism so far employed to undergird people's rights as consumers. Up to this time economic resources have been distributed on the basis of contributions to production [i.e., work]. . . . As a first step to a new consensus it is essential to recognize that the traditional link between jobs and income is being broken."[7]

The *result* of this letter—imagine that—was the National Commission on Technology, Automation and Economic Progress appointed by president Johnson (Daniel Bell was one of its distinguished members), which issued its report, "Technology and the American Economy," in February 1966, just as Heather Ross was writing up her dissertation proposal. It emphasized unemployment as the core issue of the time, a social problem that was impending yet unavoidable as an economy still geared to war evolved, inevitably, into something less martial.

Here, already, the goal was the end of welfare. In claiming that purpose, the commission cited proposals from Milton Friedman and James Tobin—in other words, proposals for a guaranteed annual income from both Right and Left.

The commission called it "income maintenance," as would the social experiments sponsored by the OEO which followed: "The Commission recommends also that Congress go beyond a reform of the present structure [of taxation] and examine wholly new approaches to the problem of income maintenance. In particular, we suggest that Congress give serious study to a 'minimum income allowance' or 'negative income tax' program. Such a program, if found feasible, should be designed to approach by stages the goal of eliminating the need for means test [*sic*] public assistance programs by providing a floor of adequate minimum incomes."[8]

So by the time the House of Representatives voted for Nixon's FAP in April 1970, a bipartisan, practically universal consensus was composed of these assumptions:

1. The end of work was in sight because private enterprise could not create enough jobs to sustain anything approaching full employment, and thus could not maintain aggregate consumer demand for a growing output of goods and services.

2. Any transparent or intelligible relation between work and income, between the production and the consumption of goods, had been erased by technological innovation.

3. One way or another, public spending would have to make up the deficit in aggregate demand, and *recreate* a transparent or intelligible relation between production and consumption, by means of (a) existing welfare programs, and/or (b) direct employment by government, and/or (c) income maintenance (transfer) payments to households or individuals.

4. Income maintenance (c), or a guaranteed annual income, was the best alternative to existing welfare programs.

5. Any income-maintenance program would have to include both strong incentives to work and robust

provisions for child care if it were to pass the test of public opinion and the vote of elected representatives.

V

The future of work looked bleak from the vantage point of the 1970s, whether viewed as a moral tablet or an economic indicator. From either perspective, it looks a lot worse now.

The future these intellectuals, politicians, and policymakers had glimpsed was a world without work and the psychological renunciations that went with it; but instead of ignoring its disturbing *and* liberating implications, as the Left and the Right of our time seem determined to do, they *mapped* this world. In what they called the "automation" and "cybernation" of goods production, they saw both the threat and the promise of a social order unmoored from—unanchored by—the daily demands of necessary labor.

Still, unlike contemporary politicians, academics, journalists, and intellectuals, whether liberal, conservative, or radical, they didn't turn away from either the threat or the promise. In their view, "full employment" was a receding horizon, almost a hopeless dream, not a self-evident purpose, and they acted accordingly.

The world these people glimpsed is the reality of our time.

But back then, full employment was not the uniform answer to the moral questions and economic issues attending the problem. Journalists, academics, intellectuals, and legislators agreed instead that neither private enterprise nor the government could create enough remunerative jobs. So they searched for *alternatives* to work—they tried to decouple income from occupations.

We ought to be in the same hunt. Of course we can (A) try to create more jobs by whatever means, public or private, and move toward "full employment"—meanwhile hoping that a more intelligible, more justifiable relation between work performed and income received is created as a result. Or we can (B) acknowledge some obvious facts, as did the people who either conducted those social experiments or voted for Nixon's FAP in 1970.

Plan A is unrealistic for two reasons. First, private investment can't serve the purpose of job creation on the scale necessary, no matter what contemporary economists say about its importance. There aren't enough tax incentives to get the banks and their corporate clients off their asses, and the combined capital/labor-saving quality of recent technological innovation will limit the employment effects of whatever private investments do get made. Second, public investment on the scale necessary can't be mustered by a gridlocked Congress—or by any Congress.

As I will suggest in the next chapter, Plan A is also punitive, in the sense that it requires everyone to get up and go to work when we can already produce more than we need with less and less labor time.

Plan B, which would be titled "Fuck Work" if it were a program, is both more realistic and less punitive. It doesn't require more investment, either private or public. Instead, it requires a minor readjustment of budget allocations and priorities, so that the funding of entitlements and transfer payments is placed on a permanently sound footing (abolishing the upper limit on Social Security contributions, which now stands at $113,700, is a start; taxing corporate income at a reasonable rate is an even better next step).

Plan B proposes that everyone will work less, not more, in keeping with the steady increase of labor productivity and the correlative tendency toward the zero marginal cost of labor. So it guarantees a minimum annual income to every citizen, on the assumption that there's no way to calculate a justifiable relation between hours worked and dollars earned.

Plan A presumes that work must continue to create the character and determine the income of each individual, regardless of how few "good jobs" have survived the past hundred years of technological innovation. Plan B acknowledges that work can't serve these purposes because there's just not enough of it, and that we need, accordingly, to look elsewhere for the sources of these essential elements of personal identity and social standing.

There's not enough work to employ most adults at a living wage because we've become so productive that the relation between work and income is arbitrary in any case. As a result, we need to find new ways to justify and new means to enable the consumption of goods—ways and means that aren't determined by the money we make from our jobs.

In other words, Fuck Work.

TWO

Labor and the Essence of Man

I

Perhaps you're not surprised that a guaranteed annual income became a live option at the end of the fabled 1960s, when anything seemed possible. OK, but now ask yourself this question: Why did it disappear so quickly in the 1970s, to the point where the findings from the Canadian experiment—which matched up with the American precedents—were actually suppressed by the provincial government of Manitoba?

Or ask the same question another way: How did this once mainstream idea become the exclusive property of left-wing radicals—the so-called Autonomists in Italy, for example, about whom more later—or Silicon Valley futurists, to the point where, by now, it appears as a *utopian* program with no intellectual purchase on the real world?

You can't explain this exclusion by citing a *conservative* backlash, the Reagan Revolution and all that. America's so-called turn to the right is greatly exaggerated. Since 1980, the Left (again, broadly construed) has won every battle it has chosen to fight, from civil rights, voting rights, and women's rights to queer equity, despite what Reagan and the Republican Party have accomplished by parliamentary procedure or jurisprudential decision or "massive resistance" — that is, by the same means the slave power used to sustain its backward civilization before the Civil War, the same means the former Confederate states have since used to stymie social progress. The Left is now winning the battle it belatedly joined on economic inequality, forcing the 1 percent to justify its privileges on preposterous grounds.

No, Nixon's Family Assistance Program stalled in the Senate because *liberals* were suspicious of its supposed work requirements. On these grounds, for example, social workers, the most liberal of interest groups, became the most outspoken critics of the legislation. These work requirements were in fact minimal. But they were a necessary part of the ideological package Nixon was selling; for a substantial bloc of voters — not just the Chamber of Commerce — worried that the working poor would quit their jobs and loaf around all day if given the chance. A Gallup Poll in 1968, for example, showed that 58 percent of Americans opposed a guaranteed annual income of $3,200 to a family of four; the typical sentiment reported by this majority was "nobody should get something for nothing."

George Shultz, the secretary of the Treasury, addressed these issues in testimony before the House Ways and Means Committee in October 1969. He began by saying that "Work is a major feature of this program." But he quickly moved to head

Labor and the Essence of Man

off liberal objections by explaining that only a third of recipients would have to register with the local public employment office, and that less than 1 percent of those who did would be "disqualified" from Family Assistance Program eligibility. He emphasized throughout his testimony that *poor people wanted to work*, anyway. (The data from the ongoing New Jersey experiment would validate this claim.)

In a follow-up letter to Wilbur Mills, the all-powerful chairman of the House Ways and Means Committee—it's a letter that is both astonishing and poignant in view of today's parochial attitudes toward the issue—Shultz insisted that to get people off welfare and into the workforce, the federal government had to subsidize "quality child care," exactly as Nixon's FAP proposed to do. Otherwise, he explained, any incentives to get up and go to work would be cancelled by the costs of private-sector day care.

He was of course correct, then as now. But, like Rumsfeld and Cheney, he was Nixon's henchman. Again, *what were they thinking?*

The advocates of Nixon's FAP—Shultz, Rumsfeld, and Cheney among them—knew they were up against public opinion, which equated "welfare dependency" and a guaranteed annual income. But they also knew that the welfare system was broken, *and* that a crisis of unemployment was waiting on the other side of the Vietnam War, when massive military spending would no longer buttress the economy. So they were willing to experiment with an alternative to welfare that decoupled income from work.

That's the big difference between then and now. Politicians still whine about welfare—everybody does—but these days nobody's willing to discuss the merits of a guaranteed income, except in the arcane terms Milton Friedman coined, as a "negative income tax," or in the equally arcane terms the Autonomists and the futurists deploy to peddle their postwork Utopias. And this whining takes place as the crisis of unemployment foreseen by Nixon's henchmen gets worse and worse.

Instead of a guaranteed income, the battle cry we hear from both Left and Right is "full employment." Both sides deploy the same slogan *to avoid the economic and ethical implications of more "entitlements"*—to get people "off welfare" and into jobs—because, unlike the advocates of Nixon's FAP, they believe that private investment and/or government spending can create enough jobs to put everybody back to work.

More important, they believe that *work is self-evidently good for us.*

Why? Why are we stuck in this punitive place from which reality has departed—the place where there must be a job for every "able-bodied individual," even though we don't know how to create enough of them, and where having a job is a good thing, no matter how pointless, dangerous, or demeaning it is?

The short answer is the great romance of work, which I mean as metaphor but not hyperbole—after all, we *love* to work, and we prove it every day by showing up at shitty jobs, where we can demonstrate that we're willing to make our own way in this cruel world. It's not just external, economic necessity that drives us. Something else is at stake.

What else is there? It's not very complicated. We work because as we do so we can see the changes we're making in the world, on the world, and this vision, derived from an infantile but nonetheless indispensable notion, is what we call freedom — the ability to be causative, to reshape the inherited conditions we didn't choose, to remake ourselves and the world at once.

But if that is true, if work means freedom as well as bondage, I can't just say, well, socially necessary labor is receding — jobs that pay a living wage are disappearing — so let's all forget about work and its pleasures, its rewards, its benefits. I have to explain that *something else*, that surplus of meaning we find in our jobs and vocations. How, then, to diagnose the *psychological* imperatives that keep us at work, proceeding on the assumption that every symptom is an attempted cure?

And, more to the point, how to imagine an alternative set of imperatives that would let us relax and be less productive? That question boils down to a big one: Can we imagine a different human nature?

II

Sigmund Freud was right, love and work are the two essential ingredients of healthy human being as such. He was also right to recognize these twinned urges as drives, almost instincts, that are transhistorical — every human being has felt these needs, one way or another. The "compulsion to work," as he named it, never quits, and love moves us no matter what stage of civilization we're in.

But romantic love as we understand it today would be incomprehensible to most human beings before the nineteenth century. Until then, the assertion of an individual's sensual appetites was either impossible—most people were bound by familial obligation or class position to marry advantageously and locally—or had almost nothing to do with affection and mutuality. Satisfying these appetites was a matter of paying prostitutes if you weren't an aristocrat, or acquiring lovers outside of marriage if you were. You had to make sure that whatever property you owned would be safely transferred to your heirs. So marriage was a moment in the maintenance or acquisition of social standing—a transaction with as much erotic charge as an invoice. Love as we experience it had nothing to do with such contractual commitments.

That's why, say, Shakespeare's *Romeo and Juliet* makes no sense unless you realize that the author was worried about the deadly results of the star-crossed lovers' single-minded pursuit of their "violent delights"—their sexual satisfaction. He was pretty sure that this assertion of sensual appetites, modern love, was dangerous to life, limb, and social order, among other things: the four main characters die and their city becomes the scene of civil war because Romeo and Juliet repudiate all the traditional bonds of kinship in pursuit of their passion: "Wherefore art thou Romeo? Doff thy name, take all myself," she exclaims, and Romeo responds accordingly, as if that name, his family, every tradition that bound him to obey his own father, these mean nothing—until he is exiled, and then he knows he is nothing without them. We moderns can identify with these lovers, though, because Shakespeare was also sympathetic enough to their new agenda of unbridled individualism to portray them as smart, funny, and resourceful enemies of the ancien régime, the place where fathers got to decide on the allocation of everybody's sexual energies.

In the nineteenth century, novelists like Jane Austen, Emily Brontë, and George Eliot would continue to remark and lament the opposition of love and marriage—but they would also depict it as a difference that might be narrowed by granting women a choice in the matter. Still, love as their characters experience and express it must feel formal, disciplined, and ritualized by comparison to our contemporary standards, if only because the range of choice for all parties to the bargain was so limited. In short, modern love is nothing like its predecessors.

The same thing goes for work. Karl Marx was right to declare, in volume I of *Capital* (1867), that the labor process, the metabolic exchange with Nature we call work, was transhistorical: "It is the ever-lasting Nature-imposed condition of human existence, and therefore is independent of every social phase of that existence, or rather is common to every such phase."[1]

Marx was also right to suggest that the *perceived* continuity of human existence, and so the very idea of human nature and history, was imposed on us by the requirement of work in the form of purposeful, social labor—*as against the instinctual foraging of animals*: "Because of this simple fact that every succeeding generation finds itself in possession of the productive forces acquired by the previous generation, which serve it as the raw material for new production, a coherence arises in human history, a history of humanity takes shape."[2]

But the meanings and possibilities of work have changed profoundly since human beings began recording their accomplishments, just as they have with love. So when Marx and Freud treat work as a self-evident property of being human, even as the defining characteristic of human nature, we need to step back, to ask if that was always the case. And if it still is.

I wouldn't issue the warning—or ask the question—except that this once novel view of the matter has finally become common sense in thinking about the future, from Left to Right. As such, it's finally become an intellectual problem, a real constraint on fresh thinking about the place of work in the world as it is, not as we would like it to be.

The question, as we might now phrase it, is, can love as we know it survive the end of work?

III

As a first approximation of an answer, let's take a closer look at the meanings of work as they have evolved in historical time—to see if they can help us get over the fundamentalist faith in the worth of human labor that Marx and Freud perfected.

I use the word "faith" advisedly. This fundamentalism started out as a religious principle that sustained the intellectual momentum of the Reformation. Marx derived his belief in

Labor and the Essence of Man

the centrality of work from G. W. F. Hegel, the great German philosopher of the early nineteenth century: "He grasps labour as the essence of Man," as the young Marx put it. But Hegel himself cited Martin Luther as the primary source of his own willingness to equate work and self-consciousness, the highest achievement of the human spirit.

At any rate Hegel treated the Reformation, particularly Luther's notion of a "calling"—a real vocation, a worldly purpose that served God's—as the turning point in thinking about the meaning of work. The modern era began, according to this specification, when "the repudiation of work no longer earned the reputation of sanctity," as Hegel explained in *The Philosophy of History*. That was when Luther told his congregations to "stay in your callings, there the Devil will lay cross enough upon you": there, while you're at work, he will teach you that the condition of grace is engagement with this world, not abstention from it.

Before then, socially necessary labor was understood by everyone—not just the philosophers and the priests—as the lot of slaves and serfs, underlings all. Freedom and its correlates, including the ability to attain the truth by reasoning, required exemption from the demands of economic necessity, from work itself. You couldn't even think for yourself, let alone virtuously or "objectively," on behalf of the common good, if you were beholden to another for the material rudiments of mere survival. As a slave or a serf, you didn't follow your own inclinations, you did your master's bidding: you had relinquished your will, you had sacrificed your volition to his, not because you wanted to but because you had to, to avoid death or destitution.

The exception to this rule in the ancient and medieval world of the West was the skilled labor, you might even say the omnicompetence, of the craftsman, the artisan, the freeholder. The work these men performed went by the name of *poiesis*, as in "making" or "composition"—as in *poetry*. It was creative work and it was *unforced* by a master. So its performance created intellectual as well as economic independence, and therefore the possibility of citizenship. If you were independent in this twofold sense, you couldn't be coerced or duped by the wealthy men who lived off the labor of slaves and serfs. You were your own boss, as we would put it today: you answered to nobody.

Centuries later, Ralph Waldo Emerson and Abraham Lincoln spoke this same language. In "Man the Reformer," a lecture first given at a library founded by mechanics' apprentices in 1841, Emerson introduced what he called the "doctrine of the Farm." He sounds like an innocent ancestor of Hannah Arendt, Richard Sennett, or Matthew B. Crawford in doing so—in saying that "every man ought to stand in primary relations with the work of the world, ought to do it himself." He wasn't pretending. He believed in work of this very specific kind, artisanal or craft labor as we would now call it, *poiesis* as the ancients knew it. "Labor is God's education," Emerson wrote, "he only is a sincere learner, he only can become a master, who learns the secrets of labor, and who by real cunning extorts from nature its sceptre."[3]

Now listen to Lincoln as he addressed the Wisconsin Agricultural Society in 1859. Lincoln here set out to prove that there was "no permanent class of mudsills" at the North, no proletariat forever consigned to penury under the rule of capital, as the

Labor and the Essence of Man

slaveholders at the South kept saying. He insisted that social mobility was the rule, not the exception, because wage earners would keep rising from the ranks of mere proletarians to become proprietors in their own right. "Many of you independent men, in this very assembly," he said, "were just last year hired laborers." Nobody asked him to clarify that statement because everybody in his audience understood exactly what he meant.

Like the apprentices Emerson addressed, the men in Lincoln's audience understood, to begin with, that freedom meant self-ownership: you were independent, not subject to the dictates of wealthier men, if you owned what made you human, your capacity to produce value through work. As a hired laborer, you relinquished your own free will for the time he "rented" your skills. Your employer hadn't bought you outright, as a slaveholder could, but this time spent working for another was still an encroachment on your autonomy — it was an infringement of your liberty, because it wasn't time spent doing what you wanted to. So you might have called it "wage slavery," in accordance with the usage of, say, the Workingman's Party of New York, which made a name for itself by denouncing capitalists.

But this term as a hired laborer was a temporary, thus tolerable condition, by Lincoln's account — and his was typical of the mid-nineteenth century — because you could save part of your wages and, within a few years, buy a farm or start a small business, becoming, as a result, the proprietor of your self, becoming an independent man because *your time was now your own*. The property residing in your capacity to produce value through work had reverted to you, as it were, because you no longer had to sell it in the labor market. You were finally your own boss.

This notion of social mobility is still at the heart of the American Dream, no matter how you define it, even though we long ago decided that wage labor is nothing like chattel slavery—or most of us have decided that, anyway. We're still attached to the idea that hard work will bring appropriate or commensurate monetary rewards, and that these rewards represent higher rungs on the social ladder. More important, we're still attached to the idea that hard work is intrinsically good for us because it produces self-discipline and self-respect.

In other words, we still believe in the principle of *productivity*: from each according to his or her abilities, to each according to his or her production of real value through work.

IV

Again, these are emphatically modern ideas. Ancient philosophers and medieval Christian theologians would have scoffed at them, or been bewildered by them. They assumed, with good reason, that anyone trapped in necessary labor wouldn't have the time to study the appropriate texts—the canonical scriptures, whether *The Iliad* or Genesis—that determined what could be thought about this life and the next. They knew that the good life happened *absent* work, or *after* death, when the intolerable weight of required exertion, particular circumstance, and everyday existence was lifted.

In this sense, theirs was an aristocratic ideal, available only to those with enough property or income to afford *leisure* time, in abstention or release from necessity. Or, among Christians, it was an otherworldly ideal, appealing only to those with enough faith to believe in the reality of a heaven that would follow from life experienced as mere probation on earth. Until the Reformation, most people believed that heaven *on* earth was the Land of Cockaigne, the peasant utopia satirized by Pieter Bruegel the Elder in 1567 as the place without work, where food fell from the trees and milk flowed in the streams.

The Protestants—the men and women like Bruegel who made the Reformation—repudiated *both* ideals. Neither the good life nor the Kingdom of God happened absent work, they insisted, or after life on this earth. These were instead the dimensions of mundane existence, the effects of "warrantable" callings in the here and now. Work was where you became your truest self, and the profane world was where you found redemption. In Thomas More's *Utopia* (1551), for example, no one is idle: disciplined social labor makes earth into heaven.

Two centuries later, at the height of the evangelical revival in the American colonies known as the Great Awakening, an uneducated, itinerant preacher who would help found Rutgers College, young Gilbert Tennent of New Jersey, explained and justified this Protestant reversal of the relation between the sacred and the profane: "To trust the Care of our Souls to those [ministers] who have little or no Care for their own, to those who are both unskillful and unfaithful, is contrary to the common Practice of considerate Mankind, relating to the Affairs of their

Bodies and Estates [their property]; and would signify, that we set light by our Souls, and did not care what became of them."

The world was turned upside down by this attitude, just as the well-born and the well-educated had feared, in the sense that hereafter the church itself—its doctrines, its priests, its rulings—would be judged by its constituents from the standpoint of their everyday lives, not the other way around. (Keep in mind that the Catholic Church was the most powerful political entity in Europe, and that the chief prelate of the renegade, "protestant" Church of England was the head of state, the king himself.) Religious sanction for conduct good or bad became pointless—the otherworldly standards of the sacred could no longer help anyone assess the possibilities of profane life. Every man was his own priest, his own savior, and no man, regardless of his lineage or his wealth, was free of the obligation to work.

The Protestant work ethic was, then, something more democratic, more radical, and more consequential than a blueprint for an ascetic personality, or a handy excuse to drive lazy peasants off the commons, away from the carnival, and into the factories. For it criticized, even excoriated, those who lived off the labor of others, as parasitic growths on the body politic—nobody should get something for nothing—and it insisted that the rewards of work on this earth ought to be distributed *here and now*, not in some hereafter. As such, this work ethic created the moral universe we still take for granted—the one where, because "all men are created equal," consent is the only viable principle of political obligation, and justice, not majority rule, is the only acceptable rationale for the exercise of state power.

That ethic wasn't imposed on peasants and workers by the conquering bourgeoisie. The people who believed most fervently in it, then as now, were themselves producers of goods who worked industriously, but without the external discipline of the factory. They were the artisans, the skilled workers, who became Chartists in London, or Luddites in the Midlands — the men who made good on their rage against the machines by breaking them — or they were the constituents of the Workingman's Party in New York, radicals all. They resisted what they perceived as the degradation of work, not work as such. But the unskilled proletarians who succeeded them, those who constituted the permanent working class Lincoln couldn't acknowledge as an impending reality, were no less committed to work as the means to the proper ends of self-respect, self-discovery, and social mobility.

Nor are we any less committed. And that's our problem. We've long since gotten over any quasi-religious, otherworldly ideal that would store the fruits of our labor on the shelf of an afterlife. Meanwhile, that ancient, aristocratic ideal of the good life as release or abstention from necessary labor *is now within our reach* because the end of work is now within sight.

But we cling to the Protestant work ethic anyway. What's even more remarkable is that the Left is more interested than the Right in the redemption of work according to Protestant specifications — through (1) "full employment"; (2) workers' cooperatives; (3) trade unions; and, above all, through (4) the revival of craftsmanship, that is, the ancient ideal of *poiesis*.

In the next chapter, I claim that each of these distant echoes of the Reformation is a belated, and quixotic, attempt to restore the dignity of work. Their saving grace is of course the shared assumption that if human labor is sanctified, the great majority of human beings will be empowered. But these Lutheran echoes are no less constraints on our thinking about the impending future than the fundamentalism of labor perfected by Marx and Freud.

THREE

Love and Work in the Shadow of the Reformation

I

Because the Left (broadly construed) still lives in the shadow of the Reformation, it's no less dedicated to the redemption of socially necessary labor than were Luther, Hegel, Marx, and Freud. Nietzsche and Weber, the other dead German guys we still read, were more doubtful about the salutary effects of a work ethic. But if we read closely, we'll detect ambiguities in Hegel, who worried about the "slave morality" residing in the "deferred desire" work always requires; in Marx, who came to believe that real freedom came after work; and in Freud, who, like Hegel, understood that the remainder of the Protestant work ethic was the symptom of repression, perhaps even regression.

Before we get to those ambiguities, let's see how the contemporary Left recapitulates the intellectual imperatives bequeathed us by the Reformation.

The progressive advocates of full employment, for example, from Dean Baker and Jared Bernstein to Thomas Edsall and

Mike Konczal, frame their proposals as alternatives to working-class *dependence* on the dole—in other words, as a way of balancing the budget, heading off the growth of entitlements, and quieting popular (not just Republican) fears of a "nanny state." If people have jobs, the argument goes, they're not on welfare, so they're not just absorbing tax dollars taken from hardworking citizens. Instead, they're in a stronger position to bargain for better wages and working conditions on their own account. Here is how Edsall, the *New York Times* columnist, summarized the progressive political morality of full employment in December 2013:

> The economics of survival have forced millions of men, women, and children to rely on "pity-charity liberal capitalism" [Edsall is here quoting Konczal]. The state has now become the resource of last resort, *consigning* just the people progressives would like to turn into a powerful force for reform to a *condition of subjugation*—living out their lives on government subsidies like Medicaid, the Earned Income Tax Credit, and now Obamacare.[1]

The only alternative to this vaguely, benignly fascistic version of liberalism, according to Edsall and Konczal, is a "bold" public policy commitment to full employment, presumably because more jobs mean less dependence on the state for income supplements, aka transfer payments, entitlements, and government subsidies.

Now, Edsall and Konczal are no reactionaries. Neither are Baker and Bernstein. By any political measure, these are genuine progressives—they're left-wingers all. And yet the implications of their argument are profoundly conservative, because they suggest that income without work, whether that means getting an old-fashioned transfer payment like Social Security or a guaranteed income, is of dubious moral value.

Notice, to begin with, how the welfare state appears in Edsall's paragraph exactly as it does in Paul Ryan's Republican dream world, as the oppressor of the poor—an insatiable bureaucracy that produces *dependence*. Then notice how a potential "force for reform" is made pliant, docile, and inert because it doesn't just receive, it *relies* on government subsidies. If you didn't know any better, you'd think a Tea Party enthusiast wrote this paragraph after finishing *Atlas Shrugged*, particularly in view of the reference to Obamacare as a government subsidy that will subjugate the poor, to be sure, but also create a permanent constituency for the Democrats, the party of "pity-charity liberal capitalism."

From this standpoint, there's no middle ground between work, on the one hand, and dependence on the other—between having a job and being subjugated by the state (or the party).

But let's grant the advocates of full employment their most basic assumption, that a "bold public policy commitment" to job creation through public spending is only a *temporary* expedient that can be dismantled once a normal rate of growth returns, post recession. What if a normal rate of growth produces no new jobs? What then?

It's not a rhetorical question. The recession has been officially over for six years, as corporate profits and stock market prices have soared, but employment has never recovered—there's been no net gain in jobs. Where do the jobs come from here-after? If government spending is the *permanent* answer, the people employed as a result will be no less dependent on the state (or the party) than those now consigned to a "condition of subjugation" by the new ward heelers of "pity-charity liberal capitalism." What follows?

In these historical terms, the practical question can't be how to put people back to work, but how to detach income from employment.

II

The contemporary advocates of workers' cooperatives and trade unions are no less Protestant (or Hegelian, or Marxist) in their insistence that work is the essence of human nature—and so must be protected against the degradation of wage labor, on the one hand, or protected by contractual agreements (collective bargaining), on the other.

It's clear at any rate that the American version of the movement for cooperative workers' ownership is intellectually grounded in more than the grand success of Mondragon, the huge worker-owned enterprise in Spain that has astonished the world with its efficiencies. In the United States, this movement is also inspired by the nineteenth-century antislavery argument that there could be "no property in man"—the argument that one's capacity to produce value through work is an *inalienable* element of being human, a natural right that can't be bought or

Love and Work in the Shadow of the Reformation

sold. From this standpoint, even the temporary "rental" of that innate capacity according to the terms of labor contracts (formal and informal) was, and is, no less unnatural and unthinkable than slavery.

Why? Because responsibility for your actions "cannot be transferred like a commodity" to another, as David Ellerman, the principal theorist of the cooperative movement in the United States puts it, even if your actions are determined by the terms of your hire: a paid assassin is no less liable for murder than the man who hired him. In this sense, wage *labor* is not much different than wage *slavery*, and human liberation therefore requires the abolition of a system in which most of us work not for ourselves but for others, for incomes alone rather than the intrinsic rewards of work.[2]

Ellerman's first principle and fundamental finding is that the rental of a person is no less fraudulent and absurd than the ownership of one. In a book called *Beyond the Corporation: Humanity Working* (2011), David Erdal explains Ellerman's thinking in a striking way:

> In the employment contract the employee is rented. In theory and in legal terms the employee is treated as a thing, an instrument — like a rented car. But actually a person cannot be turned into an instrument — cannot be rented by someone else any more than he or she can be owned by someone else. . . . In more theoretical terms, autonomy is inalienable. That is not a normative statement about how things ought to be, but a factual

one about how things are [*sic*]. . . . It follows that the employment contract is in fact a fraud.[3]

These ideas have deep roots in nineteenth-century labor movements, as well as in antislavery arguments. Here, for example, is how the Knights of St. Crispin, the shoemakers' union, explained its opposition to wage labor and its embrace of industrial cooperatives in 1870:

> We claim, that although the masses have advanced toward independence [there's that word], they will never be completely free from vassalage until they have thrown off the system of working for hire. Men working for wages are, in a greater or lesser degree, in the bonds of serfdom. The demand and supply of labor makes them the football of circumstances. . . . We cannot expect to overcome this law of supply and demand; yet we believe, that in proportion as a man becomes his own capitalist, in the same degree does he become independent of this law. How all men can become their own capitalist, is a question already decided by political economists. The answer is — *cooperation.*

Christopher Mackin runs a consulting business out of Cambridge, Massachusetts, Ownership Associates, which acts on these very ideas by showing workers *and* employers how they can deal with the prospect of plant shutdowns or hostile takeovers — or friendly buyouts by large corporations — through the creation of employee-owned enterprises, that is, cooperatives pretty

Love and Work in the Shadow of the Reformation

much as the Knights of St. Crispin envisioned them. He tells me that 11 million Americans currently work for such enterprises, more than are represented by the AFL-CIO. He sees the possibility of what he calls "democratic capitalism" in the growth of employee-owned corporations like Harpoon Brewing, whose founders recently created an Employee Stock Ownership Trust (ESOP) and sold their company to its workers instead of taking a more lucrative offer from Budweiser.

I asked him about the cooperative ideal he promotes. Does it exalt the moral significance of work to the point of fetishism, in good Hegelian fashion, thus distracting us from the possibilities, moral and otherwise, of life absent or after work—when we function as consumers, say, or as flaneurs, what William James called the "ideal tramp," rather than makers, doers, producers?

"No," Mackin said. "We're trying to democratize the workplace because we think the experience of work is fundamental, for better or worse. We're not nostalgic for the age of the artisan, small business, and all that. We want employees to understand that they can control this crucial part of their lives by owning it." I pressed him on this. So you want participatory democracy at work? People taking responsibility for everything they do, on the job and off? "Yes," he said. "Because that responsibility isn't something you can alienate, anyway. You can't sell it, and you can't rent it either. You can only *delegate* it."

The key issue for the cooperative movement is what the philosophers call "human flourishing," the cultivation of one's innate capacities as the path to self-knowledge. Here's how

Mackin explained this notion in solid, practical, and yet Aristotelian terms to Erdal: "I'm interested in human development, the effect on personality, the way employee ownership can build healthy non-intimidated human beings, people who have a place to stand, from where they can deal with the frictions and fears and roiling emotions that arise in hierarchical social life. A democratic firm properly structured has the best chance of being a community of equals."

So—as against Marx—Ellerman, Mackin, Erdal, and their colleagues argue that the buying and selling of labor power is an illusion, a legal fraud perpetrated by political theory, on the one hand (John Locke is the pivotal figure here), and by the Anglo-American tradition of common law, on the other. In this sense, they follow the lead of the Workingman's Party of New York and the early, utopian socialists (Pierre-Joseph Proudhon is the exemplar), who, unlike Marx, treated property as *theft* and the creation of a labor market as a catastrophe. In the same sense, they follow the lead of ancient authority, Aristotle in particular, by enlarging the scope of the participatory ideal to include the workplace.

But they are nonetheless with Marx (and against Aristotle) in assuming that the essence of human nature is the capacity to produce value through work, and deducing from this axiom both a body of theory and a set of practices. To that extent, their cooperative ideal, intriguing as it is, precludes fresh thinking about the possibilities of a world in which work is no longer the central, formative event in our everyday lives.

The advocates of a strong labor movement as the obvious

and necessary agent of progressive change also assume that work is of the human essence, and, to that extent, they, too, operate within the common sense created by Hegel, Marx, and Freud. Once upon a time, from the 1930s to the 1960s, these advocates were major players in policy-making circles because between them, the AFL and the CIO created a powerful political presence able to hold its own against the Chamber of Commerce.

No longer.

In the past forty years, trade unions have almost disappeared, to the point where only 10 percent of workers bargain collectively according to negotiated contracts; manufacturing jobs in steel and autos, the heart and soul of the new labor movement invented in the 1930s, have been exported to low-wage, non-union regions, including the American South; employment increases have been concentrated in white-collar occupations, which are notoriously inhospitable to union organizing (at least as abetted by the courts); temporary and contingent labor have become the norm in the design and allocation of office space as corporations themselves come and go in a quickening spiral of mergers, bankruptcies, relocations, or rebrandings; and technological change now threatens to erase most of the job classifications the Labor Department has used for a half century to calculate employment patterns and trends.

In this situation, it's perverse to claim that "the" working class is the obvious, indeed the only bearer of progressive hopes. It would seem even more perverse to claim that the nineteenth-century tradition of labor republicanism —

the tradition exemplified by the Workingman's Party and the Knights of St. Crispin — contains a political theory or practice adequate to the twenty-first century. And yet leading liberal and left-wing intellectuals, for example Alex Gourevitch in a brilliant new book called *From Slavery to the Cooperative Commonwealth* (2015), and Steve Fraser in a celebrated new book called *The Age of Acquiescence* (2015), make both claims as if they're self-evident.

The liberal and left-wing advocates of full employment assume that the bargaining power of workers, and thus their inclination to organize, will increase as the supply of jobs does. Meanwhile the advocates of labor republicanism and workers' self-management via employee-owned enterprise assume that everybody's identity is necessarily a function of his or her role in the production of goods and services. And the even more left-leaning, avowedly socialist advocates of a labor movement galvanized by new organizing drives assume that only a militant working class can change things for the better.

They're all unlikely prisoners — or is it guardians? — of the Protestant work ethic.

III

But the real trustees of this system, the ones who keep us comfortable in the prison house of work, are the people who have written most passionately, eloquently, and convincingly on behalf of *craftsmanship*. It's a distinguished company. There's no point in exhuming the entire intellectual genealogy, from

Aristotle to Arendt, but we do need to see how political philosophers and professional historians have shaped our thinking about work. I'm not suggesting that everybody has read their books — of course we haven't, I'm claiming instead that we take their ideas for granted, treating them as self-evident truths, just common sense. I'm also claiming that we need to free ourselves from their grip.

Some of these writers are almost household names — Hannah Arendt, Richard Sennett, Christopher Lasch, Jackson Lears. Some of them have been fugitives from academic respectability — Lewis Mumford comes to mind — and some of them, like Alain de Botton and Matthew B. Crawford, still are. All of them are brilliant defenders of the ancient ideal of *poiesis* (although, to be fair, de Botton is more ambiguous than the others about the meanings of work).

Arendt is the key figure. When she wrote *The Human Condition* (1958), a book originally funded by the Rockefeller Foundation as a critique of Marx, she spanned all the continents that mattered in western philosophy — she had been Martin Heidegger's student in the late 1920s, but, unlike most other refugees in flight from Hitler's Germany, she admired the intellectual energies of her new home in the United States. (Her best book was *On Revolution* [1962], which claimed that the American Revolution was far more successful and significant than the French version.) She was Sennett's Ph.D. adviser at the New School for Social Research in New York, and she inspired Lasch and Crawford, among many other writers, to defend an ancient work ethic against its modern alternatives.

So conceived, the great irony and the real value of *The Human Condition* reside in the same split: Arendt wrote an impassioned defense of *meaningful work* at the very moment socially *necessary labor* had become subject to technological erasure through automation. She knew it, and she said it:

> The modern age has carried with it a theoretical glorification of labor and has resulted in a factual transformation of the whole of society into a laboring society. The fulfillment of the wish, therefore, *like the fulfillment of wishes in fairy tales*, comes at a moment when it can only be self-defeating. It is a society of laborers which is about to be liberated from the fetters of labor, and this society does no longer know of those other higher and more meaningful activities for the sake of which this freedom would deserve to be won. . . . [Even] among the intellectuals, only solitary individuals are left who consider what they are doing in terms of work and not in terms of making a living. What we are confronted with is the prospect of a society without labor, that is, without the only activity left to [us]. Surely, nothing could be worse.[4]

Her task, as she saw it, was then to rehabilitate work (*poiesis*) and political action as the "higher" activities that could occupy us as we passed beyond the realm of necessity—beyond socially necessary labor—so that something more than spastic consumption of worthless goods would characterize our daily lives. Like every pre-Hegelian philosopher and almost all post-Hegelian social theorists (including Marxists), Arendt measured the modern world against ancient ideals and found it empty, crass, ridiculous, even disgusting. So she often wrote as if her complaints were self-evident. For example: "Viewed as part of the world, the products of work [again, *poiesis*]—and not the products of labor—guarantee the permanence and durability without which a world would not be possible at all."[5]

If I understand what she's saying here, I want to laugh out loud. She can't be serious. But she says it again and again, always more emphatically. For example:

> The only activity which corresponds strictly to the experience of worldlessness, or rather to the loss of the world that occurs in pain, is laboring, where the human body, its activity notwithstanding, is also thrown back upon itself, concentrates on nothing but its own being alive, and remains imprisoned in its own metabolism with nature without ever transcending or freeing itself from the recurring cycle of its own functioning.

(Arendt is riffing on Heidegger's notion of "worldness," from *Being and Time* [1927], in a way that is consistent, I think, with his postwar essays on humanism and technology, and that is also constitutive, I believe, of Elaine Scarry's meditations in *The Body in Pain* [1985].)[6]

Now if you've ever worked in a factory, on a grounds crew, at a construction site, or as a janitor—I've had all these crappy jobs—you know better than this. You know that what seems mindless, merely manual labor, is never just that, and that it can't be: only animals and psychopaths remain imprisoned in their own metabolism, which is to say bound by the physical drives we call instincts. You also know the paradoxical result, which is that, unlike most human beings, animals and psychopaths remain uniquely individual in their final articulation as sentient beings, at the hour of their death.

The rest of us work with others, and with our minds in high gear, no matter how menial the task, and when we die, a carnival of mourning begins, unless of course we have renounced the world. All our lives, we engage in *social labor*, and in doing so we transcend or free ourselves from the recurring cycle of the bodily functions specific to us *as individuals*.

You're never alone on the job, even when you're all by yourself. Don't kid yourself, writing is the most social kind of labor, because it presupposes the conventions of language, form, and style, but it also requires storage and distribution systems that transcend the boundaries of every individual's imagination, in every century. And no matter how eccentrically you have fashioned yourself, you don't die alone, either.

At any rate, that has been my experience, and more to the point, that was Hegel's argument in the famous master-slave section of the *Phenomenology of Spirit*: the slave, not the master, achieves self-consciousness because he's able to transcend his abjection, to defer his immediate desire for liberation from bodily pain by transforming the external world through work. The master is *in* but not *of* this world—unlike the slave, he doesn't have to engage it, and change it, and so he can't know it, or know himself.

Arendt's depiction of "laboring" in *The Human Condition* is therefore an explicit retort to Hegel, and, at another remove, to Marx. By her antique accounting, the master, the man removed from necessity, is the model of self-consciousness.

But where does that leave us? How can I invoke Hegel and Marx after criticizing them as primary sources of our fetishistic devotion to work? I do so because the master Arendt conjures is the intellectual, the philosopher-king, the craftsman of other people's lives—the writer who knows how to *represent* others, "the people," to tell the story of the rest of us. He's not the man of leisure Plato and Aristotle posited as the guardian of virtue, however, because when they wrote, "the people" were the unwashed rabble, unworthy of representation except as comic relief.

What goes missing in Arendt's accounting is just this, *the rest of us*, the men and women of leisure who have already been created by the development of capitalism. That category would include most of us, and I do mean most. I mean those without jobs; those whose jobs have been minimized ("downsized") by technology; those who have steady jobs but not enough income (Walmart "associates," adjunct professors, fast-food workers); and those who have jobs that afford them little money but enough time to permit the pursuit of a vocation (teachers, journalists, professors).

We all have something in common, and that is the opportunity —I almost said luxury—to think of ourselves as something other than an *economic function*, something more than an occupational designation. Something beyond work, after work, outside work, anywhere but at work.

Arendt's fear was that when liberated from the constraints of laboring, we would waste our time—leisure would corrupt us, make us the dupes of televised ambition and rural idiocy, which have converged in our own time as reality TV. She never considered the possibility that we would know better than to retreat to the idiotic, inarticulate state of worldlessness.

But here's the thing. After Nixon's FAP, neither has anybody else considered this possibility, as a practical question or an impending reality. Not Christopher Lasch in *The True and Only Heaven* (1991), not Richard Sennett in *The Craftsman* (2007), not Matthew Crawford in *Shop Class as Soulcraft* (2009), not Alain de Botton in *The Pleasures and Sorrows of Work* (2010). Nor Robert and Edward Skidelsky in *How Much Is Enough?* (2014). Nor the Autonomists, the mostly Italian theorists inspired by Antonio Negri, who grasp that information technology has fundamentally changed the nature of work, and could abolish it, at least as we know it—not even their heiress apparent, Kathi Weeks, in *The Problem with Work* (2009).

Instead, everybody wants us either to be working or to have *meaningful work*. Otherwise, they assume, the superficiality and hedonism of consumer culture will contaminate us, and we'll become the creatures of the demagogues who promise us more of whatever's available.

Take Crawford's new book, *The World beyond Your Head* (2015), for example, where he recapitulates the intellectual itinerary of his 2009 best-seller (*Soulcraft*) by insisting that manual labor of the skilled kind—in a word, *poiesis*—is the cure for what ails us isolated, bumbling inhabitants of a consumer culture galvanized by narcissism (note the homage to Lasch in this charge). It's a replica of Arendt's argument and is, for that reason, no less earnest and no less laughable.

Crawford goes beyond Arendt, however, by claiming that the obstacle we face in retrieving meaningful work from the dustbin of history is that we have let ephemeral representations stand in for a reality that he insists is directly available to our apprehension. He blames the Enlightenment, the new thinking of the seventeenth and eighteenth centuries, for this needless distraction from "the things themselves." But by Crawford's accounting, the category of Enlightenment includes everybody from Newton and Locke to Vico, Descartes, and Kant—in this sense, he's up against modernity as such. He's also against *representation* itself, the urge to *mistake* one thing for another that we call metaphor, the linguistic capacity that makes us human. How can that be? Here's a sample of the polemic:

> Whether you regard it as infantile or as the highest
> achievement of the European mind, what we find in Kant
> are the philosophical roots of our modern identification
> of freedom with choice, where choice is understood as
> a pure flashing forth of the unconditioned will. This
> is important for understanding our culture because
> thus understood, choice serves as the central totem of
> consumer capitalism, and those who present choices to
> us appear as handmaidens to our own freedom. When

the choosing will is hermetically sealed off from the fuzzy, hard-to-master contingencies of the empirical world, it becomes more "free" in a sense: free for the kind of neurotic dissociation from reality that opens the door wide for others to leap in on our behalf, and present options that are available to us without the world-disclosing effort of skillful engagement.[7]

As if freedom, whether understood as release from social constraint and political dictate (this would be the modern, liberal, "negative" rendition) or as access to political power (the ancient, republican, "positive" rendition) doesn't produce choices? As if the world is disclosed to me only if I use my body in skillfully engaging it through manual labor? As if the craftsman, the artisan, is still the only model of knowledge, and the only site of authenticity, available to us? Give me a fucking break.

Hegel, by contrast to Crawford and Arendt—and everybody in between, particularly Sennett—made his way beyond *poiesis* in *The Philosophy of Right*, the treatise that completed the journey begun in *The Phenomenology*. Here, in paragraphs 67 and 80, he explicitly stated that wage earners were not slaves, and that the property made legible and actionable in the control of one's own body *after hours* was the first embodiment of freedom.

In *The Phenomenology*, he had already ridiculed the slave morality of the "beautiful soul"—the Stoic, the Skeptic, or the Christian who would insist that his freedom was a private matter of conscience, not something to be substantiated in public,

Love and Work in the Shadow of the Reformation

at the law, in civil society, or at work. In doing so, Hegel was claiming that Augustine, the saint who insisted that "in interiore homine habitat veritas [in the inward man dwells truth]," was too good for this world.

Or not good enough for the modern world.

Marx followed Hegel's lead. On the one hand, he suggested that the liberation of the working class would require its abolition as a class—once freed of their chains, after all, proletarians wouldn't be workers (employees) anymore. On the other, he announced that true freedom lay somewhere beyond the realm of necessity, somewhere outside the domain of socially necessary labor. "The realm of freedom does not commence," he said, "until the point is passed when labor under compulsion of necessity and of external utility is required."

Herbert Marcuse, the Frankfurt School philosopher, took this idea as far as it could go in his brilliant, heartbreaking meditation on Marx and Freud, *Eros and Civilization* (1955). Unlike many, perhaps most Marxists, Marcuse understood that Marx himself was arguing *against* work as an appropriate aspiration for a social movement adequate to its time, "the modern time" as Hegel would have it. Like many, perhaps most social scientists of the 1950s—and like Arendt—Marcuse saw that the forces of automation would soon reverse "the relation between free time and working time on which the established civilization rests." Unlike Arendt at this very moment, he looked forward to "the possibility of working time becoming marginal, and free time becoming full time."

So did Kenneth Burke, my favorite literary historian. He

wasn't a Marxist, but he drew deeply on Marx to explain not just the economic crisis we call the Great Depression but the intellectual limits of the Left's response to it. Twenty years before Marcuse suggested that socially necessary labor time was an endangered species, Burke argued that whether it was or not, the ideological returns of celebrating work as such—or "the worker" as the essence of human being—were already diminishing. At the American Writers' Congress sponsored by the Communist Party in 1935, he said: "There are few people who really want to work, let us say, as a human cog in an automobile factory, or as gatherers of vegetables on a big truck farm. Such rigorous ways of life enlist our *sympathies*, but not our *ambitions*. Our ideal is as far as possible to *eliminate* such kinds of work, or to reduce its strenuousness to a minimum."

In these Marxist terms, American workers who identify as "middle class" aren't suffering from false consciousness —they're not "prisoners of the American dream," as the fatuous Mike Davis and his sponsors at *New Left Review* like to think, and as most leftists still believe. These workers are eminently rational beings who refuse to be defined by their occupations or their *economic functions*, who don't want Davis's intellectual condescension, and who don't need anyone's political representation.

As for Freud, well, he's a special case. He knew the "compulsion to work" was a symptom of neurosis, but as the founder of psychoanalysis, he rightly tried to treat every symptom as an attempted cure. His colleague, Sándor Ferenczi, went even further by suggesting that the infantile "experience" of

Love and Work in the Shadow of the Reformation

omnipotence—the creation of physical, material effects by means of sounds, gestures, magic words—was the source of the desperate human desire for freedom: work was its reenactment under the sign of the reality principle. Social labor was the sublimation rather than the simple repression or displacement of that fantasy.

But as Norman O. Brown, the great psychoanalytical philosopher of history, has shown, this sublimating urge is, in fact, a drive to produce a surplus—it's the psychological origin and the social manifestation of what I earlier called the principle of *productivity*. As such, it's the objective correlative of what Freud called the anal-compulsive character, and of what Max Weber called (at exactly the same moment) the ascetic personality.

These are both variations on the theme of the Protestant work ethic, and, by now, they are both sicknesses unto death: they're killing us by demanding more saving, more growth, and more goods as the obvious cure for what ails us. Once upon a time, this ethic empowered commoners, enabled peasants, enfranchised workers. Now it's a fetter on the development of the forces of production. It chains us to a past we don't have to relive: it's a repetition compulsion.

So how, then, can the symptom, the compulsion to work, function as an attempted cure? Only by releasing us, finally, from the drive to produce a surplus, to defer gratification, to save for a rainy day. Only by allowing us to comprehend that by now most of our labor has become socially *un*necessary—that is, work with little, diminishing, or no value in the labor market.

Only by showing us that hard work is hard time, nothing more, nothing less.

When we understand that simple fact, the criterion of *need*—from each according to his or her abilities, to each according to his or her needs—can modulate, and perhaps replace, the principle of *productivity*. At that point, we can say "fuck work" and mean it. In the next chapter, I explain how and why we've reached this point.

FOUR

After Work

I

I said at the beginning of this book that the labor market had broken down along with all others. I meant that it doesn't work as we expect and need it to—that it no longer allocates opportunities and incomes in ways we can understand or justify, unless we happen to be bankers or gangsters, occupational profiles that have recently become indistinguishable.

The Great Recession made this breakdown seem sudden; but in the case of the labor market, it's been a slow-motion collapse since the 1950s, just as Daniel Bell, Hannah Arendt, Heather Ross, and Wassily Leontief predicted, and just as the sponsors of Nixon's Family Assistance Program—Donald Rumsfeld and Dick Cheney—understood.

If I'm right about this breakdown—and of course I am, the evidence is by now overwhelming—the crisis we face is much more than economic. Because then productivity can no longer be the Measure of Man, or of men, or of anybody else.

Because then our question becomes *not whether but how* to be our brother's keeper. Can we love each other for real, by foregoing the principle of productivity and applying the criterion of need—from each according to his or her capacities, to each according to his or her needs?

If Freud was right about love and work as the essential components of human nature, what is to be done about the decline, and now the practical disappearance, of socially necessary labor? Put it this way: Can we love our neighbors as ourselves in the absence of work that supplies a living wage?

So our questions are these. How can we provide incomes for: (1) People who work hard but *don't produce value* that has a marketable numerator, by which I mean a return on their investment of labor time, among them [a] fast-food workers, journalists, academics, filmmakers, and musicians, but also [b] people whose labor time has been historically undervalued or redlined due to race or gender. (2) People who *don't* work because they *can't*, for example elderly men and women, who constitute a growing proportion of every developed nation's population. (3) People who *don't* work—they don't produce value the labor market might recognize—because they've got better things to do?

So conceived, the breakdown of the labor market is not just an economic crisis; it's a moral opportunity to rethink our relation to work, and to think anew about what, and who, we can love. But for the moment, let me frame that opportunity as yet another question. Does this breakdown signify the failure or the success of capitalism?

II

Call it a failure. Eduardo Porter of the *New York Times*, not exactly a radical economist, did just that in a column of April 21, 2015, where he bracketed the question of corporate morality —is it fair to pay McDonald's employees $8.00 an hour when the company's executives "earn" about three hundred times that?—and said this:

> The job market—that most critical institution of capitalist societies, the principal vehicle to distribute the nation's wealth among its people—is not working properly. This raises a fundamental question: If the job market cannot keep hardworking people out of poverty and spread prosperity more broadly, how will it be done? Is public assistance our future?[1]

In a word, yes. The job market can provide neither enough work nor enough income to the vast majority of those who actually want a job, and yet the surfeit of goods available in the market just keeps growing. So our choices are limited. Either we expand transfer payments—"public assistance," "entitlements," call it what you will—to allow families and individuals to make ends meet and to buy those goods, or we watch as American society becomes an ugly oligarchy, the "rich and poor man fray" predicted by Herman Melville in 1876.

Either we detach income from work, or we kill ourselves, figuratively and literally. Either we guarantee everyone an income, regardless of their productivity, or we declare ourselves brain-dead.

But how did we get to this point of *moral* bankruptcy, where you can't buy the right not to die unless you have two jobs or work on Wall Street—where you're either on the dole or dead to the world? To answer that question, you have to switch sides with me and call the breakdown of the labor market not a failure but capitalism's greatest success.

The signature feature of capitalism was the creation of a market in labor power—in other words, the invention of a working class, a social stratum unlike any before it, with no rights to the commons and no standing as citizens. Neither slaves nor serfs, these men and women owned only themselves, or rather their capacity to produce value through work. That was all they had to sell, and they made the most of it: they changed the world.

The creation of this new class took at least two hundred years in England, from the late sixteenth to the late eighteenth century. The same social process was recapitulated in North America more quickly, between the 1740s and the 1870s. Karl Marx called it "primitive accumulation." By this he meant the dispossession and displacement of a peasantry with once customary rights to the commons—land nobody owned and nobody fenced off, where anybody could hunt or forage—and the conversion of every natural artifact, particularly land and labor power, to a fungible commodity with a market price. (In North America, this dispossession and displacement goes by the name of "Indian removal"—exterminating the indigenous people, or isolating them on "reservations.")

The key word here is the commons, the place where legal

After Work

possession, the assertion and enforcement of individual property rights — "enclosure," they called it — was inconceivable until the sixteenth century, because everybody knew that without access to the common land, you couldn't stay alive unless you started stealing or started working in the sense we moderns know, as a wage laborer.

So conceived, capitalism arrived when and where the universalization of the "commodity form," as Marx liked to call it, was completed, when even the essence of human nature, work itself, was on sale — when your worth to the world could be measured by how much it cost to feed, clothe, and house you. When labor power became a commodity, your value as a worker was the cost of the inputs — food, clothing, shelter — that allowed you to stay alive. But Marx himself, a ferocious critic of capitalism, always emphasized that wages, the index of this value, included "a historical and moral element" that exceeded the market's impersonal calibrations.

So he rejected the notion of an "iron law of wages," which predicted that as the value of labor power declined in accordance with population growth — more supply + less demand = lower price — workers would inevitably be driven to a subsistence level of existence, into what we would now call poverty. There were too many countervailing forces, Marx thought, like trade unions, social movements, and the common sense of human decency, which stood athwart the market's laws of supply and demand.

Moreover, and more important, he agreed with David Ricardo in thinking that the introduction of labor-saving machinery would of course displace skilled workers, but that overall demand for labor would nonetheless increase, *because somebody had to build the machinery.*

Still, the labor theory of value Marx perfected held that the wage rate was a mathematical function of the market costs of labor power, give or take the marginal effects of that "historical and moral element." And in formulating his so-called law of capital accumulation, he predicted the gradual extrication of human labor from the process of goods production—to the point where labor time became worthless because the machines would build themselves. In this at least his prophecies came true.

III

But what if Marx was both wrong and right? Wrong in the sense that the iron law of wages seems to be working, after all—just look at how many people with jobs can collect food stamps—but right in the sense that the "historical and moral element" in the determination of wages seems now to be making a comeback, at the very moment that labor time has become worthless? Isn't that exactly what the movement for a \$15 minimum wage is about, this reassertion of a moral urge to reject the market's equation between factors of production and human beings?

These sound like merely rhetorical questions, I know, but they're not.

The development of capitalism has reached the point of

what I have elsewhere called "primitive disaccumulation," and what Jeremy Rifkin has called the "zero-marginal cost society." He and I are describing pretty much the same thing, but our lexicons illuminate different pasts and determine different futures.[2]

By primitive disaccumulation, I mean that the commodity form regulates a diminishing proportion of socially necessary transactions, in a *reversal* of what Marx called primitive accumulation, so that the most basic requirement of postindustrial society—information—is fast becoming more or less free of charge. Think of what you don't pay for anymore because you've uploaded some kind of file-sharing software, Napster once upon a time, now BitTorrent, tomorrow who knows? My students use Russian web sites to download books still under copyright, including mine.

Today you can download almost anything without cost, so the new commons encroaches on every sector's business model, especially music and newspapers, but also movies. Soon even higher education, the last redoubt of debtors' prison, will be free, not because the politicians will restore Pell Grants and fund state universities, but because MOOCs and YouTube will give everyone online access to the most influential academics on the planet—from Michael Sandel and Martha Nussbaum to David Harvey.

Rifkin and I agree that as the market registers fewer transactions—as we produce and distribute more goods without the mediation of money—our assessments of future economic growth, GDP and so forth, must begin to look bleak.

Leading economists such as Robert Gordon and Tyler Cowen have, accordingly, predicted the decline of innovation and the end of growth. After all, the Commerce Department can't measure what's off the books. But that's the thing about this new stage of economic development—it can't be measured by the old quantitative criteria, even though we're unquestionably producing more of what we need and want.

The creators and purveyors of information—journalists, educators, musicians, filmmakers, geeks in general—aren't working any fewer hours than they used to. In fact, we're all working harder. And we're actually more productive than ever. There's more information, more music, more movies, more images than ever, *and we ourselves produce it*, but without any rational expectation of remuneration.

We know that what we do is *worthless* as measured by the standards of the labor market, but we do it anyway.

How? When and why did "making a living" become impossible? Don't say we exported all the good, unionized jobs in manufacturing (goods production). That's not an answer, because in a postindustrial society like ours, almost all the jobs are "tertiary," that is, devoted to the distribution or maintenance rather than the production of goods, and they have been since the 1950s, just as the intellectuals of that moment predicted. Repatriating those good old jobs is no different than reliving the good old days: it's just stupid.

And don't say "cheap labor" of the imported or exported kind—poor immigrants who flood the U.S. labor market or sweatshop workers elsewhere who work for nothing—because then you've already bought my argument. Now you agree with me, that the *perfection* of the labor market, the great success of capitalism, has made work useless, pointless, an unnecessary diversion from what is important. Labor-saving machinery is portable, as China's workforce will soon discover.

IV

My answers to the question of how labor time became worthless are variations on themes Marx himself developed. To begin with, the working class has been abolished, not in its own name, and not with a bang — "the revolution" — but with the whisper of cybernation. You can't have a working class in the absence of work, or rather work that has no value in the market, and thus creates no *monetary* claim on goods available through the market. And let's face it, work without income is morally repugnant because it carries the connotation of slavery; it's a great deal more repugnant, at any rate, than income without work.

So much for workers. The capitalist class we love to hate has meanwhile been abolished by other means. Primitive accumulation created a working class by driving peasants off the land and into the cities, where they would learn to work by the clock — or die trying. By the same token, it created capitalists, bourgeois individuals who would hire labor, invest in plant and equipment, save their profits, and advertise their abstemiousness as a virtue.

For three centuries they thrived, and then, at the end of the nineteenth century, they solved a fundamental crisis by sentencing themselves to social death.

The crisis consisted of working-class triumph in the Gilded Age. I know, that's not what you learned in your history classes, but that's what happened. Between 1873 and 1896, economic growth was spectacular, unprecedented, and yet its income benefits seemed to accrue mainly, or only, to workers. This was not a secret. By 1896, many leading economists (David Wells, Edward Atkinson, Charles Conant, Jeremiah Jenks) had said as much, and the Finance Committee of the U.S. Senate, chaired by Nelson W. Aldrich of Rhode Island, had convened hearings to verify and explain the anomaly.

The problem back then was the *exact inverse* of what we see today— *ours is not a new Gilded Age.* In our time, labor productivity keeps rising, real wages keep falling, and so inequality deepens. In the late nineteenth century, real wages rose while productivity stagnated (again, even though economic growth was spectacular). The measurable result, back then, was a shift of income shares from capital to labor—a profit squeeze that turned capitalists into public servants, by their own accounting and all others. Do the math. Between the early 1880s and the late 1890s, non-farm real wages rose roughly 35 percent, due mainly to price deflation; meanwhile, productivity rose only about 6 percent. This is the opposite of what has happened in the United States since 1975.

What was a capitalist to do? Bribe a senator, charter a trust, hire a private army, fall back on sport and culture—you know, get all athletic, and build museums in your spare time. Capitalists tried practically everything in the 1880s and 1890s: pools, trusts, Pinkertons, lockouts, armed violence, also wilderness resorts and monumental repositories of the visual arts bought in Paris, Rome, Florence, Madrid, maybe London . . . . What finally worked was the corporation, a bureaucratic solution to a social-economic crisis. By means of this impregnable legal device, capital was finally able to subject labor to real, as against formal, control, and productivity surged, to the point where, by the 1920s, the output of goods increased without any measurable increase of inputs, whether of labor or capital.

Notice: the corporation succeeded by reducing socially necessary labor—what the scientific managers called "the human element"—to nothing. Or almost nothing. The increase of productivity in automobile manufacturing was 400 percent between 1919 and 1929; the net loss of jobs in manufacturing for the decade was 2 million.

But the corporation was built on the separation of ownership and control. In effect, capitalists sentenced themselves to social death by turning basic decisions about production and distribution over to salaried managers who do not own the company's assets—just as their aristocratic predecessors had rented out the land to commoners, mere peasants, when faced with the social crisis of late feudalism, and thereby had sentenced themselves to a similarly slow social death.

These salaried managers act in the name of capitalism, but they are not themselves capitalists. They're functionaries, servants, courtiers, who will do anything their invisible masters decree because they have no self-determined purpose except bigger bonuses.

Consider that for a moment — savor this miraculous fact.

The end of capitalism as we knew it is already upon us. The people who benefit from the way we organize production and distribution has shrunk to a tiny, cossetted minority, the 1 percent as we now say. We don't need them, and they know it. That is why their courtiers and hirelings now seek to protect their privileges by any legislative means possible, from voter ID laws to fast-track trade treaties.

Or put it this way. The historic function of capitalists — and, more generally, class society — was to reorganize and compel social labor, to *force* men and women to be more productive than they would be, or could be, under the social relations specific to earlier modes of production, slavery or feudalism. The slaughter bench of primitive accumulation, enclosure, and industrialization is the proof of that compulsion.

By now, however, this compulsion is simply unnecessary. Our prosthetic doubles, the machines that can reproduce themselves, have made possibility rather than necessity the central fact of our lives.

That horizon of possibility first appeared in the 1920s, when the value of capital — past labor time congealed in the material form of plant and equipment — began to decline along with the value of labor, when capital-saving innovation allowed economic growth without saving or net investment for the first time in human history. In the two decades after 1920, *net additions to the capital stock were nil.* And yet economic growth was spectacular in the 1920s, and, at least between 1933 and 1937, even more spectacular (you read that right, the New Deal worked). It wasn't on paper. It was real growth, of productivity, output, and per capita income.

At that moment, profits became worse than pointless, and with them, capitalists.

Because if their historic function was to compel social labor, to extract surplus value from the working class, and to convert that surplus—profits—into investments that would determine the future (creating jobs, infrastructure, etc.), after 1920 this function was moot. Capital-saving innovation let corporations finance the improvement of their productivity and output out of depreciation funds rather than profits: the *mere replacement and maintenance* of the existing capital stock, no net additions necessary, fueled growth.

At that point, the function of capitalists and their appointees became speculation in markets that could absorb the pointless profits generated by capital-saving innovation (the stock market back then, the housing bubble in our own time). They had become a fetter on the development of the forces of production. So they could be realistically depicted, by F. Scott Fitzgerald and John Dos Passos among others, as an effete, debauched aristocracy—superfluous people.

Now, you can't have capitalism without a proletariat or a capitalist class—if the social classes that constitute it have dissipated or decayed to the point where we can't actually identify them. But that is our condition.

So we have to rethink the compulsion to work, the social and psychological territory magnified by the rise of capitalism. Why do we have to work? Well, of course, to buy the right not to die—to make enough money to get by, and, beyond that, to raise a family, to buy a home, to buy a gun or a car or a motorcycle, to attain some social standing, to have some choices and be able to demonstrate *to others* that you can make them. The principle of productivity on which capitalism once thrived is still formative. From each according to his or her production of real value, durable goods, to each according to the market value of his or her labor time: you get what you pay for, and you pay for what you get.

N. Gregory Mankiw, the remarkably naive Harvard economist who has advised George W. Bush and Mitt Romney, among others, precisely expressed that principle in a paper called "Defending the One Percent"—who could make that up?—which recently appeared in the peer-reviewed *Journal of Economic Perspectives*: "According to this view [his view], people should receive compensation congruent with their contribution."[3]

Well, OK. But what, exactly, are the gangsters on Wall Street contributing, and now that I mention it, to *what* are they contributing? Also, how is their compensation congruent with their contribution? Aren't they the people who brought us financial disaster in 2008, destroying trillions of household savings in the process? We should reward them for their idiocy?

And the fundamental question remains: Why do we *want* to work? I have asked almost two hundred people this question, in conversation and in formal interviews, and the answer is pretty much the same. Let me emphasize that these weren't all academics or intellectuals, although individuals of this persuasion were most emphatic in claiming they couldn't live without meaningful work.

I spoke with bartenders, janitors, waitresses, nurses, fast-food workers, programmers, engineers, actors, lawyers, doctors, morticians—yes, more than one—editors, secretaries, manual laborers, cabdrivers, musicians, athletes, doormen, teachers, salesmen, bricklayers, managers, currency analysts, stock traders, dentists, hygienists, carpenters, plumbers, contractors, club owners, concierges, postal carriers, and prostitutes. (The list is incomplete.)

And what was their uniform answer? A reason to live, which typically translated as a reason to get out of bed and to do the right thing while awake. They wanted something to do, somewhere to go, a place—more than that, actually, an *emotional destination*—that would help them translate their inchoate, inarticulate desires into a coherent, regular, recognizable set of meanings, and that would, accordingly, give their humdrum, everyday lives some durable shape, some significance. The answer was never "just for the money," not even when I asked the morticians and the prostitutes.

The job always appeared as a means to other ends, as it must be in a market society, but the ends were invariably an *escape* from a previous life or a *commitment* to a different life. Their regulative desire was to become somebody else, to find a future that wasn't already determined by their social origins or inscribed in their own bad decisions.

So Frédéric Lordon, a French economist and the author of *Willing Slaves of Capital: Spinoza and Marx on Desire* (2014), sounds perfectly ridiculous when he declares: "Of all the factors at work in maintaining the relation of employment dependence, market alienation is no doubt the strongest. . . . And the stage of mass consumption must be reached for the full scope of the Spinozist statement 'they can imagine hardly any species of joy without the accompanying idea of money as its cause' to become clear."[4]

Of course "they" can imagine such species of joy. No, *we* work, we engage in social labor, for the same reasons we try to love each other as ourselves—we think it will make a difference. At this historical juncture, though, the labor of love has finally become the only work available.

Listen to Mr. Conyers, a mortician from the Roy L. Gilmore Funeral Home in St. Albans, New York (it's a kind of suburb in Queens). I asked him how he could deal with dead bodies every day, and he said this:

What I do is important. I want the relatives to remember this person as she lived, what she looked like while she was alive. I don't want 'em staring and thinkin', "She

After Work

looks good for a dead person." I want 'em to see her as if she's gonna wake up, not gone forever. I learned this my first try, when Mr. Gilmore let me loose. It was a little girl, a beautiful child, run over by a car, what do I do? I put her in purple because her mother said it was her favorite color, and everybody said "Oh, my God, it's her!" I bring people back to life, you see what I mean?

He wasn't talking about the dead people.

Or listen to El, the presiding spirit of the Last Drummers, three guys who set up on the long reaches of the A Train, between 125th and 59th Street, on Manhattan's West Side. "Yeah," he says, "on the train it's definitely work, we hope for the money there, but, you know, we gonna do this anyway, that's the music, it's what we gotta do. We hear a new beat, we have to play it. Or we at a party, we know the drums come out at a certain point, everybody waitin' for it to happen. How did you say it, yeah, it's a 'calling.'"

Or Shari, the economist from the World Bank who now works for the United Nations. She gets paid a lot better than Mr. Conyers the mortician and El the drummer, but she speaks the same language: "I work because I have to; if I don't do this, what happens? Maybe nothing and that's not acceptable. I like to think that what I do is important. But I think that everybody needs this, this, what, this *purpose*. You have to have a goal, something worth doing, otherwise you don't get out of bed. Then what?"

Or Charlene the hooker, who patrols the neighborhood

bound by 125th and Lexington at one end, 124th and 3rd Avenue at the other: "I don't do this because I like it; I got a daughter in school. But look, I'd rather suck your dick than wait on you in Applebee's, get paid shit for bein' polite to you, you see what I'm sayin'?"

Or Ephraim, the window installer, once upon a time an athlete, a pitcher drafted by the Chicago Cubs who never made it to the big leagues: "I tell my daughter, you gotta do what you love to do; the money don't matter when you get to be my age. I played ball, now I do this. I'm not proud of it. But I'm alive."

Or Mel the super, who's got six buildings on my block, one of them the halfway house next door, where morons and murderers go to pretend they're not. He's a man who's always at work: "I'm blessed because I don't ride that raggedy-ass subway to the Bronx anymore" — he used to be a mechanic for the MTA — "I walk out the door every morning and there I am, I'm at work on my own street, you see what I mean? I got somethin' to do, keep me busy all day, and that's a good thing. You know I'm a be here on this stoop till 8:00 o'clock, cause that's my job, gotta make sure these people don't do nothin' stupid."

But *why* do you work, I ask him, and everybody else. "Well, shit, I got rent to pay," he says. "And you know, I got something to do, something to get done. That's a good feeling, you know what I mean? What I do, you can't do without me, don't matter that you don't see it — c'mon, I do most of my work before you get up in the mornin' — what matters is that I'm fuckin' doin' it. To me, I mean, you see what I'm sayin'?"

Or Terry the former journalist, at the *Providence Journal*, the

Los Angeles Times, and the *New York Times*, where he was a re-porter, a manager, and an editor until he was downsized in 2013 (after having done a stint as a digital downsizer himself). "Work is not a trifle," he says, "not to the fast-food workers in my writing class [which he teaches for free]. What looks like drudgery to you doesn't feel that way to them. Or to the undocumented nanny who loves the kids she looks after but still wants to get out from under the family that basically enslaves her."

"Me, neither," he continues, "I became a journalist because I didn't want to be Dilbert, and because I thought I could serve the cause of social justice by writing, reporting."

I ask him if he thinks journalism is over now that information is free.

"No," he says emphatically, "some information is unique, and by that I mean it's uniquely valuable."

But to whom, I ask. Nobody's paying you to teach those fast-food workers how to tell their stories. If our labor time has become worthless — it can't be "monetized," in the parlance of our time — then how do we explain or justify working for a living?

VI

Hanna Rosin has recently predicted the "end of men" as a result of the Great Recession. The phrase is playful hyperbole, of course, but the empirical groundwork of her argument is the significant decline of labor-force participation by men since 2008. What happens when men become useless because they don't work? Are women taking over the world because jobs of the traditional, masculine kind — you know, in factories, in manufacturing — are disappearing? Does the world turn upside down when the absence of work makes men superfluous?

Ask the question another way. As men are laid off from old-fashioned, goods-producing jobs because they lost their race against the machine, and as traditionally women's work — social work, health care, education — becomes the norm in the labor market, does the market price of labor time regress to the mean determined by the long-standing wage gap between males and females?

Put it in the terms the pathbreaking sociologist Arlie Hochschild proposed many years ago: Why doesn't "emotional labor" pay a living wage? Or put it this way: Has most labor time become, practically speaking, worthless, because the market can register the cost of *socially necessary* labor time and compensate its performance accordingly, but can't let us reward *socially beneficial* labor time — what has long been characterized, dismissed, or denigrated, as "women's work"?

In a word, yes. Socially *beneficial* labor has always been undervalued, or rather, it has never had a market price commensurate with its reproductive worth, and I use the word "reproductive" advisedly. Absent the unpaid (women's) housework of the new family created by primitive accumulation — cooking, cleaning, child rearing — wage labor would have been, and would still be, impossible. Labor markets, like all others, have subsisted since the seventeenth century on the *externalization* of such costs, environmental and otherwise. That is why markets need scrutiny, regulation, management, and containment, not obeisance.

In the late nineteenth century, when the family exported all its economic functions—when the household gave way to the factory, the school, the bakery, the hospital, the department store, the restaurant, as the site of consumable goods production—these once private or familial costs were taken up, or socialized, by public spending, mainly on education. An accounting of their value became possible.

But these economic functions remained undervalued by the labor market because it was still women producing the goods (goods in a material or marketable sense, yes, but more broadly goods in an ethical sense). And then, in the 1920s, the market value of labor power as such began to decline because the price of its inputs did, as capital-saving techniques reduced the costs of producing everything. Mechanization, automation, and instrumentation bent on the elimination of the "human element" from goods production actually worked.

As I've noted, the net loss of jobs in manufacturing was roughly 2 million between circa 1919 and 1929, and the income effects included a relative decline of consumer spending—which, in the absence of net investment, had already become the single most important source of economic growth. The Great Depression was the result, as I have elsewhere explained. In our own time, we're witness to an acceleration of the same social-economic vectors—the Great Recession was the result.

So, by now, most of us do women's work—if we can get it. The labor of love has superseded—outlasted—its rivals.

VII

For the past hundred years, this phenomenon, the end of work, has been imagined again and again. It's almost always been framed as a lament or a warning, something like what William Empson and Raymond Williams, two famous literary critics, tracked in recording the pastoral response to modern industry and its attendant, the modern city.

In 1999, for example, Susan Faludi, a feminist writer, published a best seller called *Stiffed: The Betrayal of the American Man*. It was illustrated throughout with black-and-white photos of working men, sailors, and soldiers from the 1940s and 1950s, as if time had stopped, or should have stopped, in the golden age of postwar, Cold War America. It retold the story Arthur Miller had given us in *Death of a Salesman*—the story of a superfluous working man—but it was now fortified with footnotes.

And there's the rub. That story of superfluous men was already a commonplace—a familiar conceit—of journalistic and artistic enterprise when Miller made it new. As I have said before, most sentient beings in the 1950s had glimpsed the end of work, and perhaps the end of men, in "automation" and then, in the early 1960s, in "cybernation." And, for that matter, when Faludi was writing her book in the mid-1990s, the depiction of a downsized Dad, the manly breadwinner, was a growth industry, as anybody who has seen *Toy Story* or *Terminator II* can attest.

In fact, it's been almost a century since we started hearing this lament, this warning, about the end of men as a result of the end of work. By now we're all familiar with what John Maynard Keynes wrote in 1930, in "Economic Possibilities for Our Grandchildren"—dozens of writers, including Rosin, have recently cited the piece as introduction to their own studies of the endings impending in the crash of the labor market.

All of them wonder how he went so wrong, predicting increased leisure, less labor time, more pleasure. They all ask, what was he thinking?

But the great irony is not that that he predicted less socially necessary labor time—he turns out to have been right about that, regardless of what we've done with the time left over—but that he wrote in the throes of the Great Depression, when the sheer brutality of economic necessity was reasserting its social and psychological hold on working people. Keynes rightly worried that we'd let that brutality govern our thinking about the future. "But, chiefly," he pleaded, "do not let us overestimate the importance of the economic problem, or sacrifice to its *supposed necessities* other matters of greater and more permanent significance."

His more fundamental concern, though, was that we wouldn't know what to do with the leisure time that came of labor-saving and capital-saving innovations. "Thus for the first time since his creation man will be faced with his real, his permanent problem—how to use his freedom from pressing economic cares, how to occupy the leisure, which science and compound interest will have won for him, to live wisely and agreeably and well."

Keynes knew the deviants, miscreants, and malcontents would be the ones to address this problem. "The strenuous purposeful money-makers may carry all of us along with them into the lap of economic abundance. But it will be those people, who can keep alive, and cultivate into fuller perfection, the art of life itself, and do not sell themselves for the means of life, who will be able to enjoy the abundance when it comes."

So he was a great deal more pessimistic, or less utopian, than his recent interlocutors have suggested. "Yet there is no country and no people, I think, who can look forward to the age of leisure and of abundance without a dread. For we have been trained too long to strive and not to enjoy."

Still, Keynes was more optimistic, or more prescient, than his most significant predecessor in pondering these issues — that would be William James, the most influential philosopher of the twentieth century (you read that right, Husserl, Wittgenstein, Heidegger, Bergson, Durkheim, Wahl, and Kojève were close readers and/or enthusiasts of James). In 1909, James delivered a lecture called "The Moral Equivalent of War," where he addressed the end of work and its less-than-promising implications for the "masculine virtues."

From time out of mind, James noted, boys had learned how to be men either as warriors or as workers. But now neither war nor work could school them in manliness. War would be too costly, and work of the strenuous, necessary kind would soon be unavailable; for it was already a world ruled by women: "a world of clerks and teachers, of co-education and zoophily, of 'consumers' leagues' and 'associated charities,' of industrialism unlimited and feminism unabashed."

A new "pleasure economy" driven by consumer demand had replaced the old "pain economy" determined by saving, striving, starvation, anything but enjoyment. What then? How to reinstate those "masculine virtues"? Why, full employment, of course!

Like our contemporaries on the Left who still worship at the shrine of work, James proposed to put all teenagers to work, to teach them something about the "military ideals of hardihood and discipline" hitherto bred in war—but instead of military conscription, they'd be drafted into "an army enlisted against Nature." There the Devil would lay cross enough upon them: they'd be sent "to coal and iron mines, to freight trains, to fishing fleets in December, to dish-washing, clothes-washing, and window washing, to road building and tunnel-making, to foundries and stoke-holes." There they would learn the lessons of necessary labor.

VIII

I say that Keynes was more optimistic than James because the economist, unlike the philosopher, wasn't afraid of increased leisure time. James's real worry in designing his moral equivalent of war was that personalities held together by the economic imperatives of work would regress to idleness or idiocy when exposed to the possibilities of a "pleasure economy" — what we now call a consumer culture. "The transition to a 'pleasure-economy' may be fatal to a being wielding no powers of defence against its disintegrative influences," he wrote. "If we speak of the fear of emancipation from the fear-regime, we put the whole situation into a single phrase: fear regarding ourselves now taking the place of the ancient fear of the enemy."

The philosopher was right in this regard. We still fear emancipation from the fear regime imposed by thousands of years of scarcity. *We still want to go to work.* The economist agreed. He was hopeful, but he was pretty sure we wouldn't know what to do with the leisure time the twentieth century afforded us because we had been emotionally starved for so long. He was pretty sure we wouldn't know how to enjoy each other — how to love each other as ourselves — instead.

Are we then consigned to what Freud named the "compulsion to work"? Are we simply unable to be our brother's keeper because getting something for nothing is just intolerable, even when we know that working for a living gets us nowhere? And suppose that we could get over the disease we call the work ethic, how would we pay for the "entitlements" that would necessarily follow, as in a guaranteed annual income?

The last, practical question is the least interesting because it's the one most easily solved. As I said in the preface, just abolish the cap on Social Security contributions and increase taxes on corporate income. All fiscal problems solved. And don't say corporations will relocate overseas if we tax them at higher rates—they've already done that, at an accelerating pace since Ronald Reagan's cuts. Also, don't speak of diminished incentives, because then you sound like a moron. Sure, CEOs wanted higher profit rates. They got what they wanted, and they destroyed the world economy, circa 1987 to 2015: We should increase their incentives?

The real question, then, is what disables us. Why can't we stop working, and, by the same token, and in the same measure, why can't we choose to be our brother's keeper?

Love and work, Freud taught us, are the essential elements of a healthy life. Why? Because they take us outside ourselves, bring us into the world, make us commit to social purposes. Love and work are sublimations, transpositions of instinctual drives we inherit from our animal past—they get us beyond the mere repression of our instincts; they move us toward the *social* labor that makes us human. They just *are* social labor.

But work can no longer serve this socializing purpose. So, as I've already said, we don't have much of a choice. And yet we can't make it.

IX

Why?

I have two answers. For women, entry into the labor force, and, in a larger sense, the discovery of meaningful work outside the home, has been the key to the kingdom of equality with men. The correlation of these social and intellectual moments is indisputable, as Linda Nicholson, among others, has insisted. Modern feminism was founded on just this, the notion that through work, women could enter the world as bearers of extra-familial identities, as abstract individuals rather than mothers, daughters, sisters, or wives.

For modern women, then, work has personal and political meanings it can't have for men (most of them, anyway). Vivian Gornick's poignant memoirs offer vivid testimony. They illustrate, no, they insist, that her difficult choice as a feminist was always between love and work. But then, go ahead, read any novel from, say, 1720 to 1890, or watch any movie from 1930 to 1990, and you'll find that love is women's work. The great refusal of modern feminism, as Gornick has demonstrated, is that very equation.

My other answer to the question of why we can't recover from the disease of work is contaminated by the category of race.

Here the return of the repressed becomes unavoidable. According to the economists who have studied the welfare state, Americans can't imagine being their brother's keeper because they think getting something for nothing is the prerogative of people of color. Transfer payments and entitlements are bound for "those people," not the thrifty, hardworking, rule-bound types, those white folks who are honored by the designation of *middle class*, whether by social standing or expressed aspiration.

So, to put it in terms made familiar by our recent culture wars, gender and race overdetermine our inability to think past work. But there's also a class component to this intellectual impasse. It becomes clear in the recent and remarkable book by Robert and Edward Skidelsky, *How Much Is Enough?*, which engages the questions Keynes asked in 1930 in the most serious and yet entertaining fashion.

The authors, father and son, lay out a program for a guaranteed annual income that is, in my view, wholly unobjectionable. But they also object to *idleness*—watching TV, hanging around, whatever. They want us to be doing something important if or when we're done with work. We shouldn't be wasting the free time made available by mechanical improvement, they insist.[5]

To which I say, why not? If our time on the job is becoming worthless, why not waste the rest of it?

Fuck work and its attendant idiocies. But love remains. We don't have much of a choice there, either. It's all that's left.

Coda

I

Can love survive the end of work? I've been asking that question all along. I guess I've been asking whether love can *replace* work—whether socially *beneficial* labor, the love of our neighbors, can replace socially *necessary* labor as the criterion we use in calculating the distribution of income and the development of character.

Of course it can. It already has, to judge by the state of the labor market.

The most basic good in a postindustrial society like ours is information, and it is now free. In other words, the labor market can't assign a remunerative value to the socially necessary labor of producing and distributing information. It's socially beneficial—but it's more or less worthless. The work goes on, but the income you might have accrued from it doesn't. Ask a journalist or a freelance writer, or a musician whose band doesn't tour.

So the question is not how to put us all back to work for a minimum wage—fuck that—it's how to detach income from time spent on the job. But look, we've already done that, too.

Wall Street bankers don't do much of anything except peddle bad paper, but they get paid millions of dollars. Teachers, professors, novelists, journalists, carpenters, musicians, and janitors do everything we say we value—they educate, entertain, they build things, and they clean up after us—but they get paid almost nothing.

Meanwhile the so-called welfare state has also decoupled income from work, but not so that you'd notice unless you, like Paul Ryan and Jeb Bush, think "entitlements" are a danger to the moral fiber of the nation. Remember, 20 percent of all household income now arrives in the form of a transfer payment from government, and every Walmart "associate" is a ward of the state, someone collecting food stamps or using the emergency room for routine health care, because he or she can't make it on the wages alone.

So it's not as if we don't know how to do what needs to be done, which is detach income from work; it's that we refuse to face the fact that it's now simply necessary to *complete* what we've already begun—which is the transition to a postcapitalist society, where wage labor neither determines nor disfigures daily life.

How, then, do we face the fact? I don't doubt the moral and political significance of a movement for a higher minimum wage, $15 an hour. But as I've said, forty hours a week at this pay grade just puts you at the poverty line (and you know you're not getting forty hours, because that would require real benefits from your employer). What is the point of a higher minimum wage, then, except to prove that you have a work ethic?

Excuse me, that's another rhetorical question. There's no good reason to increase wages by legislative fiat if the labor market is broken. But there's a good reason to *replace* that market. So what is to be done, for now, is intellectual work. Our question is, how to imagine a moral universe that isn't anchored to or limited by socially necessary labor — how we learn to accept income that can't be accounted for by reference to time on the job. To hell with full employment. How about full enjoyment? Fuck work.

II

Love and work — the two things we all want, according to Freud and every other student of human nature — have pretty much the same function in our lives. Like good teachers, they take us out of ourselves, into the world.

Love and work commit us to purposes that we didn't invent, and so they teach us to devise and evaluate our own. When we're in love, what we most want is that the person we love can become what he or she wants to be, partly because we know that this urgent desire includes us. When we're at work, what we most want is to get the assigned task completed, because we know that this is what our coworkers need — we know that this completion will free us from the commands of the past, and so let us experience the present, enter the future.

In love or at work, *commitment* is a condition, but also a boundary and a limit. It requires certain behaviors, and it precludes others. But commitment in either emotional venue doesn't necessarily mean a cancellation of your own purposes, although of course it can. The thing about love and work is that you typically feel commitment as both the limitation *and* the liberation of your own volition—as the *realization* rather than the negation of your self, of your natural talents, past effort, and learned skills.

Think about it as a musical proposition. You can't play the blues without mastering the genre, which is pretty simple—without memorizing the chords and the changes and the lyrics. But you can't improvise, make it new, become yourself as a player or a singer, without that preparation, that commitment. "Piety is not only honorable," as G. L. S. Shackle put it in explaining the Keynesian revolution, "it is indispensable. Innovation is helpless without tradition."

Love forces us to acknowledge antecedents—the physical actuality and the moral capacity of other people. You can have sex with anyone without this doubled acknowledgment, but you can't love someone without it. Broaden that dictum and you find that poor old Immanuel Kant was right, after all, in rendering the Golden Rule as a philosophical principle. To love your neighbor as yourself, he must appear to you as an end in himself, not a means to your ends, whether they're sexual, economic, or political.

To love someone is to treat him or her as a person who must be different from you, and who must, by the same token, be your equal. Otherwise you could rightfully decide their purposes for them, which would mean treating their moral capacity as absent or insufficient. Everyone would then appear to you as a slave or a child in need of your tutelage. The obvious limits of this supervisory vantage, by the way, are arguments against the idea that parental love (or God's love for all his children) is the paradigm of love as such.

To love your neighbor, to be your brother's keeper, is, then, to care for yourself, *and vice versa*. That is what we have yet to learn.

"As I would not be a slave, so I would not be a master." That's how Abraham Lincoln put it in an unpublished note to himself. Harry Frankfurt puts it differently, but no less usefully, in a book called *The Reasons of Love*: "There must be something else that a person loves — something that cannot reasonably, or even intelligibly, be identified as his 'self' — in order for there to be anything at all to which his self-love is actually devoted. . . . A person cannot love himself except insofar as he loves other things."[1]

Work seems much different than love in such perspective. A TV series like *The Office* and movies like *Office Space* or *Horrible Bosses* exist and succeed precisely because the people in charge quite realistically violate this Kantian principle, the Golden Rule. But that is why the heroes of these fictions say, "No, I would prefer not to." They're Bartleby the Scrivener all over again because they don't stand up to anybody, they don't even leave the office, no, they subvert the system by hanging around or doing something stupid.

Coda

But what these fools, our fools, keep demonstrating is their moral capacity, however bumbling it may seem to their bosses, and to us the audience — at first, anyway. They insist that they must be acknowledged as agents in their own right, as moral personalities who can steer this business, and their own lives, as well as anyone in charge. They reject what Hegel, also Nietzsche, called "slave morality," the idea that self-mastery is an interior to which no exterior corresponds. (The fascination with manual labor on reality TV, as in *Dirty Jobs* or *Ice Truckers*, has the same political valence; it's a way of saying that every man, every woman, can decide for himself or herself, without guidance from the well-groomed and the well-educated.)

Finally, love and work similarly remind us that the material artifacts of this world, whether natural or man-made, can be indifferent, even resistant, to our efforts. Here the rules of love begin to look like the laws of science — you can't make the beloved do what he or she won't, or can't, not anymore than you can bend the earth to your will. And here again that knowledge is a form of *self*-consciousness, a way of learning the limits of what we can ask of others, of the world. It's a way of asking ourselves, given this situation, what can I do about it?

Still, what becomes of love when work disappears?

III

Love and work as we know them, as the choices we make that decide who we are as individuals — these are the essential ingredients of modern times. They date from the late eighteenth century, when the notion of individualism we take for granted, as an expression of unique qualities that sets each of us apart from all others, took hold because it could, because the idea that "all men are created equal" became first a revolutionary slogan and then a cultural commonplace.

So the real question is, what happens to us when work must be love?

This absurd question is what we must answer, because work is no longer our lot. Unlike every generation before us, we can do without it, and we'll have to. We don't need to work. But if we want to survive, we have to love each other, as ourselves—we have to be our brothers' keepers.

It's not merely a moral imperative, as Kant would have it; this is a practical, economic necessity. There's not enough work to go around. We can produce more every year, every month, with less and less labor time. We lost our race with the machine, and we know the robots are coming to take our jobs and steal our emotions. That means the principle of productivity—from each according to his or her input, to each according to his or her output—is outmoded, even ridiculous, and not just because the more we produce, the more we destroy.

That principle of productivity has been more or less incongruent with reality for a hundred years; but then cultural revolutions typically take about a century. The relation between goods produced and income received has been totally unintelligible for that long, anyway, since the "human element" could be eliminated from the factories, and now from the banks and the stores and the warehouses, by electrification, automation, instrumentation, cybernation, computerization.

So, what is to be done?

The first thing we do is kill all the bankers. Just kidding; we need them to keep the books.

No, the first thing is, we think through what it means to detach income from work. Then we invent practical means of doing so. We don't have to start from scratch just because for the last fifty years, liberals, conservatives, and all those in between have been addressing the wrong issue, "full employment." Instead, we start with Nixon's Family Assistance Program, and see where it leads us.

Eventually we'll decide that, in the absence of jobs that pay a living wage, even at a minimum of $15 an hour, we have to provide everyone with a guaranteed annual income, regardless of the work they do. Then we get to ask the real questions.

Like, why should I love God better than this day? What do I want to be when I grow up? Where's the remote?

ACKNOWLEDGMENTS

I wrote this book under duress. My old friends made me do it. The most important of these are Bruce Robbins and Mike Fennell, with whom I have argued for many years over the questions about work I raise here. Larry Lynn, an even older friend, saved me from certain idiocy at a crucial moment, at the point two people we both cherish were threatening to die on us. (They lived, us too.) He was amplifying an argument against the book's title that Scott Goodman, a new friend, had made a year earlier.

Correspondence and conversation with Christopher Mackin and David Ellerman educated me in the best sense. We've kept our differences along with our friendship. The same goes for James Oakes and Omar Abdul Malik.

Spirited debate with Shari Spiegel made me rethink passages and positions I thought were already set in concrete. So did accidental conversations on the subway with morticians and musicians. At the last minute, Catherine Liu had the same good effect on me.

On the street where I live, my neighbor Melvin Alexander has been a constant source of insight on the meanings of work. So has Terry Schwadron, another neighbor. I quote both of them in chapter 4.

Jeff Sklansky and Nelson Lichtenstein invited me to their respective places of work to present some of these ideas. Leon Fink, of the University of Illinois–Chicago, was a remarkably acute interlocutor when I spoke there. Allan Needell was, too, as the host of a session at the Smithsonian's National Museum of American History. When I finished the manuscript, or so I thought, the dangerously clever Eric Banks invited me to give a talk at the New York Institute for the Humanities, where he presides as executive director. Thanks to him and the interlocutors who showed up at his behest—they made me rewrite.

The Internet has encouraged me to keep writing about this unwieldy topic, at Facebook; at my blog, politicsandletters.wordpress.com; and at an online magazine I started in 2014, politicsslashletters.com. The rise of Jacobin, a left-wing little magazine, has too. Alex Gourevitch, Peter Frase, Seth Ackerman, and Kathi Weeks have written powerful, provocative essays on the meanings of work at this venue. I've never met them, and I certainly don't agree with them, but I'm grateful to them for making me think harder and for their indefatigable labor on behalf of a better future.

My agent, Lisa Adams of Garamond, and my editor, Brandon Proia of UNC Press, worked long hours to get this short book published. Brandon has an uncanny ear that heard what I didn't; I'm glad I listened to him in revising.

Acknowledgments

My deepest debt is to Laura Kipnis, the hardest-working writer I've ever met. Maybe the best as well. Her example has been inspiring, her edits have been infuriating, and her advice has been invariably useful even, or especially, when it was unwelcome. I'm still crazy about her after all these years. This book is for her.

Not one of these people agrees with me. In thanking them here, I'm reminded of what G. W. F. Hegel, my intellectual model and principal antagonist in this book, wrote to himself in an unpublished fragment:

> When a man has finally reached the point where he does not think he knows it better than others, that is when he becomes indifferent to what they have done badly and he is interested only in what they have done right.

Damn straight.

NOTES

Preface

1. James Livingston, *Against Thrift: Why Consumer Culture Is Good for the Economy, the Environment, and Your Soul* (New York: Basic Books, 2011).

Introduction

1. Carl Benedikt Frey and Michael A. Osborne, *The Future of Employment: How Susceptible Are Jobs to Computerisation?* (Oxford: Oxford University Programme on the Impacts of Future Technology, 2013). Erik Brynjolfssen and Andrew McAfee, *Race against the Machine: How the Digital Revolution Is Accelerating Innovation, Driving Productivity, and Irreversibly Transforming Employment and the Economy* (Lexington, Mass.: Digital Frontier Press, 2011).

2. Julia Bellusz, "Nobel Winner Angus Deaton Talks about the Surprising Study on White Mortality He Just Co-Authored," *Vox*, http://www.vox.com/2015/11/7/9684928/angus-deaton-white-mortality (18 February 2016).

Chapter 1

1. H. W. Watts and A. Rees, *The New Jersey Income-Maintenance Experiment* (New York: Academic Press, 1977).

2. Gray Christopherson, *Final Report of the Seattle-Denver Income Maintenance Experiment* (Washington, D.C.: U.S. Dept. of Health and Human Services, 1983).

3. *Preliminary Results of the New Jersey Graduated Work Incentive Experiment Conducted by the Office of Economic Opportunity* (Washington, D.C.: Office of Economic Opportunity, 1970).

4. Fred J. Cook, "When You Just Give Money to the Poor," *New York Times Magazine*, May 3, 1970.

5. George McGovern and Wassily Leontief, "On Taxing and Redistributing Income," *New York Review of Books*, May 4, 1972.

6. Daniel Bell, *Work and Its Discontents* (Boston: Beacon Press, 1956), 56.

7. Ad Hoc Committee on the Triple Revolution, *The Triple Revolution* (Santa Barbara, Calif.: The Committee, 1964), 6, 10.

8. *Technology and the American Economy: Report of the National Commission on Technology, Automation, and Economic Progress* (Washington, D.C.: National Printing Office, 1966), 40.

Chapter 2

1. Karl Marx, *Capital* (New York: International Publishers, 1967), 1:183–84.

2. From a letter to a Russian friend, P. V. Annenkov, in December 28, 1846, appendix to Karl Marx, *The Poverty of Philosophy* (New York: International Publishers, 1963), 181.

3. Ralph Waldo Emerson, "A Lecture Read before the Mechanics' Apprentices' Library Association, Boston, January 25, 1841," in *Nature: Addresses and Lectures* (Boston: J. Munroe, 1849).

Chapter 3

1. Thomas Edsall, "Is the Safety Net Just Masking Tape?," *New York Times*, December 17, 2013; italics mine.

2. David Ellerman, "Rethinking Common vs. Private Property," DavidEllerman.com. http://www.ellerman.org/

rethinking-common
-vs-private-property/ (April 15, 2016).

3. David Erdal, *Beyond the Corporation: Humanity Working* (London: Bodley Head, 2011), 139.

4. Hannah Arendt, *The Human Condition* (Chicago: University of Chicago Press, 1958), 4–5; italics mine.

5. Ibid., 94.

6. Ibid., 115.

7. Matthew B. Crawford, *The World beyond Your Head: On Becoming an Individual in an Age of Distraction* (New York: Farrar, Straus and Giroux, 2015), 76.

Chapter 4

1. Eduardo Porter, "Big Mac Test Shows Job Market Is Not Working to Distribute Wealth," *New York Times*, April 21, 2015.

2. Jeremy Rifkin, *The Zero Marginal Cost Society: The Internet of Things, the Collaborative Commons, and the Eclipse of Capitalism* (New York: Palgrave Macmillan, 2014).

3. N. Gregory Mankiw, "Defending the One Percent" *Journal of Economic Perspectives* 27, no. 3 (Summer 2013): 21–34.

4. Frédéric Lordon, *Willing Slaves of Capital: Spinoza and Marx on Desire* (London: Verso, 2014), 28–29.

5. Robert Skidelsky and Edward Skidelsky, *How Much Is Enough? Money and the Good Life* (New York: Other Press, 2012).

Coda

1. Harry G. Frankfurt, *The Reasons of Love* (Princeton, N.J.: Princeton University Press, 2004).